THE BLOOD

Unless otherwise indicated, all Scripture quotations are taken from the King James Version of the Bible. (Public Domain)

Cover by James Nesbit:

"What honor to be asked to do a cover concerning the power of the blood. We wanted the cover to speak of that power, so crimson is the foundation. The wailing wall is faded across the bottom with an explosion representing the eternal power of the blood opening the quantum realm of the supernatural with the wonders of the Creator of the universe lying beyond.

"How great is our God! On the back portion of the cover we felt the need to honor the work of the cross, the blood of the New Covenant and the power of the cup." -James Nesbit

Published by CSA Publishing
P.O. Box 1017
Maricopa, Arizona 85139
Unites States of America
www.XPpublishing.com

ISBN: 978-1-936101-44-3

For Worldwide Distribution

THE BLOOD:
ENTRANCE INTO THE SUPERNATURAL

Rona Spiropoulos

THE BLOOD:
ENTRANCE INTO THE SUPERNATURAL

This is the most powerful book on the Precious Blood of Jesus that I have ever read. I have taught on this subject for decades in the nations of the world. But, never have I had the revelations that were given to this young Greek girl when she had a face-to-face encounter with the powerful Blood of Jesus in a supernatural visitation many years ago, when she was baptized in the Holy Spirit in Africa.

When we think about Jesus' Blood, we have a tendency to analyze it, like a scientist or a chemist. But we haven't the least understanding of the God-Blood that flowed in the veins of that "Man of Sorrows," the Son of God.

"Five bleeding wounds He bore" is what they taught us. But the truth is that His blood began to pour out from His pores as he travailed in Gethsemane for our souls (Luke 22:24). His face poured out blood when they pulled out the hairs of his beard from their roots (Isaiah 50:6). They tore out the skin of his back when they whipped him with the cruel Roman scourge, giving Him forty lashes (save one) by strong Roman soldiers, smashed the two to three-inch spikes of the crown of thorns on His head, blinding His eyes with the blood that fell from His bleeding head. They nailed both of His hands and His feet, and finally, when He had died one of the soldiers pierced His side with a spear, and immediately there came out blood and water (John 19:34).

In Greek mythology, the fluid said to flow in the veins of the gods consisted of this mixture of blood mingled with water. It is when this happened, that the earth shook and trembled with a great earthquake, darkness covered much of the world because "the sun refused to shine" (their Creator had died), and the veil of the Temple was rent from top to bottom supernaturally, opening the way for us to enter the supernatural realm.

Upon seeing all these things, together with this strange "blood and water" which poured from the wound in His side, *"Now when the centurion, and they that were with him, watching Jesus, saw the earthquake, and those things that were done, they feared greatly, saying, Truly this was the Son of God"* (Matthew 27:54).

So powerful is the Blood of Jesus that it has the power to redeem the sins of any soul on earth from Adam to the Millennium—if only man will accept it as the ransom for his soul.

Peter recorded in Holy Script, *"Forasmuch as ye know that ye were not redeemed with corruptible things, as silver and gold, from your vain conversation received by tradition from your fathers; But with the precious blood of Christ, as of a lamb without blemish and without spot"* (I Peter 1:18-19).

"Each drop of blood bought me a million years," sang Stuart Hamblin, when God gave him that beautiful song about the Blood of Jesus.

His life on earth was like any other man's. His body was shaped like any other man's. He lived, ate, slept, and drank, like all good Jewish men would. The only difference was in His Blood. His Blood was Divine. Therefore, it had the power to redeem souls from their sins, for it was sinless Blood. All creative power was in His Blood. It could never decay, nor lose its power. It is eternal, because it is God-Blood.

Many of God's children do not understand this, therefore they live carnal, sinful lives, often filled with bitterness, criticism against those who have had the greater revelation of the Power of the Precious Blood, and thereby have crossed over into another world.

This wonderful, little book will open a new world for you. Read it prayerfully, walk watchfully, and guard your soul against any critical spirit of rejection of end-time truths and revelations.

It is this supernatural Divine Blood that opens the door for us to enter into the supernatural.

GWEN R. SHAW, PH.D.

FOUNDER AND PRESIDENT,

END-TIME HANDMAIDENS, INC.

PREFACE

This book has been written in two parts because as I sat down to rewrite what was originally a six-lesson teaching series on the Blood of Christ, into a readable book, the Lord began to speak to me prophetically and I wrote what I heard. Some of it was beyond my own knowledge, but as I researched the facts I found them to be true. One example is in the prophetic word, "A Lamb in All His Gentleness," which says, "My Lamb lies across the skies," there is a constellation of stars that looks like a ram which is a male sheep.

I did not quite know what to do with the prophetic words originally, and after some prayer and thought they have become Part One of the book. Part Two is a "line upon line Bible Study which I pray will not only minister to you, dear Reader, but you will be able to use the study as teaching material.

As we reach the final days of time as we know it, there is going to be a greater and greater revelation of the Blood of Jesus Christ to those who pursue Him. We will have to realise its power as we walk through catastrophes and as part of the Lord's victorious army on this earth. The Blood will also be a stone of stumbling as a lukewarm, man-pleasing church talks less and less about it in order not to bring offense to the hearers.

"What can wash away our sin?

Nothing but the Blood of Jesus.

What can make us pure within?

Nothing, but the Blood of Jesus!"

Robert Lowry (1876)

This truth still stands, only the Blood of Christ has the power not only to wash away our sins but to transform us into His likeness and continually change us from glory to ever greater glory.

We welcome you now, into the pages of this book, and into the realm of your own revelation of the Precious Blood!

Father, we ask now that you would open up revelation of the Blood and of the realm that you live in to the one that is reading this book. Amen!

INTRODUCTION

I was caught up in the wonder of it! Caught up in the passion of fresh love, caught up in the fire of a love that knows no bounds. Love drew me, pulled me back when I attempted in my search to walk in a different direction, and captivated me so that I thought it was my own decision to give myself to Him.

It was 1976 and I was a Greek Orthodox girl who had just had an encounter with Jesus Christ and was Baptised in the Holy Spirit. I did not know about the gospel, I did not know about the Blood, I had heard about it, certainly, but I did not understand what it was all about. In a moment of time, I had been translated out of one Kingdom into another. Every morning the Lord would wake me up very early and I would tiptoe through the house to the living room where I would meet with Him. It became my trysting place, and there, in a series of visions, the Lord began revealing the gospel to me. One of these visions was about the Blood. I saw the Lord standing before me as I was lying, face down, on the carpet, out of His side came a fountain of Blood, which covered my whole body then became absorbed into me and I knew that I had been cleansed. I now belonged to Him.

11

If we could only understand the power of the precious Blood of Jesus, the Christ, the Anointed One of God, we would be a Force to be reckoned with on the earth and in the heavens. The enemy understands it and fears, and he does everything he can to prevent it being preached or sung about, so that we do not know what we have available to us, nor do we know who we are in Christ.

> *"Forasmuch as ye know that ye were not redeemed with corruptible things, as silver and gold, from your vain conversation received by tradition from your fathers; But by the precious blood of Christ, as of a lamb without blemish and without spot"* (1 Peter 1:18-19).

> *"For the LIFE of the flesh is in the Blood"* (Leviticus 17:11).

The story of the Blood is the story of a Life that replaced ours, an incorruptible Life that restored us again to our Father so that He could pour His Spirit into us and pour His Glory into us. Only in this way could He bring us back into intimacy with Him.

We were created for intimacy with Him.

This is God's love story.

RONA SPIROPOULOS

Part One
MEDITATIONS ON THE BLOOD OF CHRIST

TABLE OF CONTENTS

TABLE OF CONTENTS
(Continued)

TABLE OF CONTENTS
(Continued)

DO YOU TRUST ME?

*I*t is all about trust! How much do you trust Me? Have you drawn so close to Me that you know Me intimately and personally? Do you know My character, My reactions, what I feel about situations, do you understand My moods?

If you don't you are liable to believe what is wrongly taught about Me.

Can you really trust Me if you don't know Me, not know about Me, but know Me. When someone else comes to you and tells you something about My character do you believe them even if it is not true? It is all about trust, and you have to know Me to really trust Me.

My character has been slurred and maligned by My own who think I am a certain way and have taught it to others and they have been wrong. They have been sincere, but they have been sincerely wrong, because they have not spent time in My inner courts and have relied on the traditions of man.

Let Me ask you a question. If you were in the Garden of Eden and were approached by the serpent who challenged you with the same lie, what would you think of Me? Would you say, "No, I know my God and He is not like that," or would you go the way of Adam and Eve, and get caught up in a lie. Would you believe what was said about Me instead of what I showed you of Myself when we walked in the cool of the evening?

For you this is just a story, although you believe it to be true. But I lived it. I was there, I walked with Adam, My heart broke through his betrayal because he could not trust Me. You see, trust is at the heart of the matter.

Now, I ask you again, do you trust Me?

2

HEAVEN
WITNESSED IT ALL

Whenever the Blood is taught the great cloud of witnesses come to listen and the mighty hosts of angels want to hear the Word and hear about the Blood. They know that Blood was not shed for them, but they want to hear how Jesus, their Master, redeemed mankind through His Blood. They want to hear about the Lord of Hosts who is their Leader, having so great a love that He willingly laid down His life to bring many sons to glory.

"For it became him, for whom are all things, and by whom are all things, in bringing many sons unto glory, to make the captain of their salvation perfect through sufferings" (Hebrews 2:10).

A SCENE OUT OF HEAVEN'S PORTALS

The angels remember that great and terrible day, when He would not allow them to rescue Him. They waited in the Sides of the North, the true Mount Zion in Heavenly realms, to just hear a word from Him, Who was the Word, Whose Word created the planet earth and its inhabitants. One Word from Him and the Via Dolorosa would have been no more, that place of Golgotha would have been shattered; Heaven would have come down and wreaked havoc! They were waiting, silent, Heaven stood still, even the four winds were silent, still, waiting!

The angels had already seen Him whipped, crowned with thorns that penetrated into His mind and tormented Him with unacceptable thoughts of revenge, thoughts of pride, "…How dare they!" Those thoughts could not be received if He was to be the perfect sacrifice, an unblemished Lamb. In the midst of the pain that wracked through His body, He had lifted up His eyes. As He hung between life and death, He felt a longing, a desperate homesickness, a desire to go home, to just leave that tortured body and return to those He saw watching Him, loving Him and feeling every torment with Him. He longed to be with them, to be loved again. He shook Himself and focused again on the cross that waited, welcoming Him, it was growing heavy. He knew it well, He remembered it from the Foundation of the world when He was slain as a Lamb. He had to resist the urge to leave, to opt out before the work was completed. He had lost some Blood, He was covered from head to toe in His own Blood, but He had to be a poured out offering. He had to lay down His life unto death. He had to resist an early death, He had to pay the full price.

He lifted up His eyes again – this time He looked into eternity – He saw us!! He saw those that would enter into Sonship and carry the glory, which was the reason that He was shedding His Blood. He was purchasing them. He saw crowd after crowd walking through the portals of Heaven, clothed in the riches of His Kingdom, having completed their task on the earth and manifesting within themselves

His fullness. They were the glorious ones, transformed into His likeness because they had passed through the veil of His Blood and lived in a high and holy place that He had gained for them. His Blood had bought them new life and had transformed them. His Blood rested upon them like a mantle, the Light in that Blood had never dimmed. It had the power to lift a human life through the realms of Heaven and penetrate through the body to ignite the spirit. The glorious ones! They were the ones to whom the Holy Spirit had revealed Who He was and they had accepted Him in every aspect of their lives. How could He not continue His walk to Golgotha.

Jesus felt the shame of His nakedness – it was part of the price – the power of shame would be broken that day over mankind. He willingly carried it, it was laid on Him by His Father. It was a part of His cross. He would complete the task. It was worth it all. A fountain would be opened up, that fountain that waited in the Heavenlies for this moment. It was established years ago when He was slain, now it would begin to flow. He smiled, sent a nudge of comfort to His hosts of angels and continued walking...

Darkness began to gather as the hordes of hell were released, crying their victory cries as they saw God trapped in a human body being tormented and killed. They did not know that Life itself could not die nor could His Light be extinguished. They gathered and they danced through the heavens, darkening the skies, screeching their wild screams! The hideous creatures laughed and contorted creating a furor and a calamity in the lower heavens. "We have taken captive the Son of God! We will take Him down to the lower regions of Hell where we will torment Him forever!" "Ha ha ha!" they laughed. The skies darkened even more as they released the darkness of their dark world.

The angels saw all that happen, looking at each other with eyes of deep compassion, wondering how much more He would have to bear. They watched and waited! They saw Him placed on the cross and lifted high for all to see. And then it happened…His Blood began to drip onto the earth…the earth itself shuddered. His Blood was somehow different but it still looked like Light. What was it? There was something dark that was trying to extinguish the Light but could not. The darkness was trying to overwhelm Him but could not. They heard Him speak to them quietly, "For this reason was I made manifest!"

Then His voice was heard, "It is finished!" And again, "Father, into Thy hands I commend My Spirit."

His side was pierced and Blood and Water began to pour out of Him. A fountain was opened up! A fountain that was a combination of the Light, which looked like water, and the purity of His blood, which knew no sin, Blood which carried the record of a life lived perfectly.

As it poured onto the earth, the earth shuddered even more. It began to shake as the purity of the Blood affected it, shattering the effect of the curse, bringing it into release from the weight of sin. The earth began to move and stretch like a new patch on an old garment. It opened its mouth in a great cry as it reacted to the injustice that was perpetrated and gave a home to that pure Blood until it could be retrieved by the angels.

The angels turned and looked at the Father, the One Who enfolded Himself in Light; a rainbow surrounded Him, the timeless, all-knowing One. When they looked at Him they were always filled with joy, even on this occasion, nothing took Him by surprise. His Eternal Throne was never shaken! When He sent His Son to earth, He sent a part of Himself. "Man will have to suffer the consequences of this great sin, because of the intent of their hearts, but, My mercy will prove to be greater!" He said.

Just then a terrible ripping sound filled the atmosphere and shook both Heaven and earth. "Now, it is truly finished," the Father said, "that terrible veil, which was never my highest intent, has been torn in two by My own hand. Now, the people can come to Me through the veil of the shed Blood of My Beloved Son. The way has been made open!"

"The Mercy Seat awaits His Blood, then He can forever sit at My right hand, a High Priest forever, after the Order of Melchizedek, after the Order of an Eternal Life."

"And, behold, the veil of the temple was rent in twain from the top to the bottom; and the earth did quake, and the rocks rent" (Matthew 27:51).

"And the sun was darkened, and the veil of the temple was rent in the midst. And when Jesus had cried with a loud voice, he said, Father, into thy hands I commend my spirit: and having said thus, he gave up the ghost" (Luke 23:45-46).

See also Mark 15:38.

3

THE DOOR

My people stop short of what I have for them. I am not just the man on the cross with a broken body, not just a man of sorrows, but I am The Door. The veil of My flesh was torn to open up a doorway into other worlds. In My Kingdom I have always been known as, "The Gateway," "the Point of Entry," "The Entrance," "The Opening." This is because whenever any of the inhabitants of Heaven come near Me they are transported into new realms. Creative realms are opened up to them, they begin to see into new dimensions and their understanding of My Father opens up to them. They would go swirling off into universes if I were not there to keep them true.

The mystery is this: Not only am I the Entry Point into new realms; but all of those things are within Me. In Me is a realm of holiness, of the Shekinah glory that is so intense that it is beyond time and space, so anyone who comes near Me is drawn into it. Out of Me worlds are birthed, I explode with creation. It comes flaring out of Me as glory which creates new realms, new living beings, yet I hold all things together.

On the cross, the veil of My flesh was rent; it was torn in two every bit as real as the curtain in the Temple. I was covered in Blood and My Blood and My broken body became access points into the realm of the Shekinah, the realm of the supernatural, the realm of creation. Don't stop and worship Me only at the cross, but realise that the cross was the focal point of the ages, the place where Heaven and Hell met and the past and the future came together. It was a place of timelessness because I brought it all together. And then, as I was The Entry Point in My Heavenly Kingdom, I became The Entry Point on earth, The Door.

So, step through the veil of My Blood and the Light in My Blood will examine you and cleanse you. Step into a world of glory, abundance, fruitfulness and freshness, of resurrection power and timelessness. Then worship Me in the realm of eternity and there, My Father and I and the Hosts of Heaven will come and join you.

"Which hope we have as an anchor of the soul, both sure and stedfast, and which entereth into that within the veil" (Hebrews 6:19).

4

OUR OWN
HUMAN BLOOD

ow I want to talk to you about your own blood. It is
a picture of the liquid fire and life-giving streams of
Heaven. It is the liquid fire that travels through the
glorified, resurrected body of My Son. It is the Light of Resurrection
that can transmute the natural into the supernatural, the natural
into the glorious. Your own blood has red blood cells that are orbs
(discs) of congealed light. Each one has a life of its own and each one
records your personal lifestyle. The reason that redemption takes
place through Blood is that your life, everything that you are, your
sin, is carried about in your blood.

When you pass through the veil of My Son's Blood, your own
blood is transformed, the supernatural is ignited in each cell. That
is the Light of Christ. His Blood has transforming power, it is a
filter through which you are passed, your blood is passed, because
through your blood your whole life is transformed. It is known that
through medical blood transfusions the recipients can take upon

themselves the character of another. If it happens in the natural, it surely happens in the supernatural.

Your blood reaches every cell in your whole body including your heart and your brain. When it passes through the filter of the Blood of Christ, He is taken to every area of your body and transformation begins to take place. The Light of the world has come in you!

Apply His Blood, by speaking it over yourself, to every part of yourself, spirit, soul and every area of your body, and in so doing let the Light enter in to every place. This is redemption. Acknowledge that when you passed through the Blood, you left the death in your blood behind and each cell of your being has passed into Resurrection Life. This is done according to your faith. Believe that when you passed through the veil you left everything behind and that is how it will be.

The veil, the Blood of Christ, is the Entrance into the Most Holy Place where I dwell, the highest Throne Room of Heaven, the realm of highest glory. It is the place where mysteries are revealed as scrolls are opened, where you will eat of the Hidden Manna, the glorified body of My Son. This is not eating as you know it on earth, but partaking into yourself of the divine DNA for glorification. As that DNA unfolds, the recipe for glorification is given to you.

Open your heart, believe that nothing is impossible, and it will all be opened to you. The mysteries of Heaven are available to you.

5

PORTALS IN OUR BLOOD CELLS

*W*ithin every blood cell is a portal, a realm of Light, a gateway into the supernatural. Quantumly speaking, if a cell is analysed it will be found to have a measure of gold in it. This is left over from the glory that Adam had, but also, naturally speaking, that minute piece of gold is necessary for the electrical charge of life every cell gets from the blood as it passes through. This electrical charge releases nutrients and pulls out toxins from the cells.

That minute piece of gold is also the connection to the realm of the Spirit, the supernatural. When you pass through the Blood of Christ and become a new creation, your blood is ignited in a way that would be described as an electrical charge connection through the gold and it becomes glorified once again. It becomes electric with My Presence, the Presence of My Spirit, with the Godhead. Did I not say, *"Behold, I stand at the door and knock?"* (Revelation 3:20). I will come in and sup with you and you with Me. It is not only with Me but of Me in divine union. I am giving you a Blood transfusion as in covenant and I too, partake of the sweetness of your fellowship with Me.

When I knock, I knock on more than just the door of your heart as you have always thought, it means that I knock on every cell of your body, because within every cell there is a door. I want to pervade every area of you until you radiate with my glory. Only in this way will you find your true self and become what you were created to be.

If I have your life totally, it means that I am travelling around your body in your bloodstream, igniting life, bringing divine order to your cells, looking through your eyes, hearing through your ears and speaking through your mouth.

I will commune with you in this place of glory, of the Shekinah where I enter in to take My rest. I am Truth unveiled and Truth will find its resting place in you.

6

BLOOD COVENANT

*T*he Blood Covenant is all about exchange, an exchange of lives. When people see you coming they should see Me; and My Light should go before you to prepare the way for My Word to come forth. When your life is hidden in Me, you dwell in the place of communion between the Cherubim and My radiance becomes your covering in an exchange of life. My life for yours, the glory that covers me, for your world and your own defense systems.

The sword that I put into your hand will cut through chains and release the captive. It will be seen as Light coming out of your mouth and heard as sound that penetrates the enemy's prisons and strategies. In Me, you will understand the sounds that come out of My Blood and will hear the Voice of it crying out to the captives and beckoning them in. The Voice in My Blood speaks better things than the blood of Abel that cried out for revenge. The Voice in My Blood cries out for mercy!

When My Blood covers others through prayer, it begins to work to break the power of darkness off them and bring enlightenment, and then My Blood breaks down walls that have them enclosed and imprisoned. Only believe – nothing is impossible to him that believes. You can take the enemy's kingdom because there is nothing as powerful as My Blood, and nothing can stand against it.

When My Blood covers nations the angelic hosts are alerted because they hear the sound of it, they see it and they rush to that nation and begin to work to set it free from oppression. My Blood can still the voice of the bloodshed in a nation and can bring that nation to its knees but My people do not have a revelation of the greatness of it. Why don't they? Surely they realise that a transformation must have taken place in My Blood for Me to be raised from the dead. If it could raise up and glorify My shattered body, laden down with the sins of the world through all the ages, each sin being a sentence of death, the power in My Blood could raise up a nation and cleanse a world. Light shatters the darkness – only believe!

My Blood is greatly honoured in Heaven not only because of the glory in it and its great power but because it is a picture of liquid, selfless love. When the hosts of Heaven, who are not only angels, see it they are alerted.

"And to Jesus the mediator of the new covenant, and to the blood of sprinkling, that speaketh better things than that of Abel" (Hebrews 12:24).

THE ABILITY TO RECREATE

My Blood carries within it the ability to recreate. Your genes are recreated, your DNA is recreated through the process of exchange, so that we can agree together and live in union. The Blood can recreate body parts, it can recreate broken down structures of the soul, it can enter into cracks and crevices and renew and rebuild. My Blood can repair broken relationships, it can calm the wind and still the stormy sea.

I can go into the memory banks of your heart and the processes of your soul and reform and recreate and make new and fresh. Memories are like kinks in the DNA strand, which can form mutations of the original plan, so one's ability to walk uprightly and maintain a forward thrust of motion is obstructed. Memories are often so buried because of pain, that they are hidden away in iron caskets instead of being brought to the Light to be washed and refreshed and the DNA restored to God's original plan and beyond.

God's plan for each one is so high and so great that the revelation of it to each individual would not necessarily lead to pride, but would lead to the fear of being proud and thus the plan is aborted. Ask Me if you can look at the plan for your life through the filter of My Blood, in that way you will know that you are looking at absolute truth. As you continually walk in access of My Blood, you and your divine destiny will melt into each other. No lie can live in My Blood because I AM the Truth, the Life and the Way and you will find Truth, reality of Life, and the Way made open to you as you stay within the realms of My Blood. It will recreate you, straighten and strengthen your DNA and make you abundantly prepared for your destiny and all that is involved with it.

Try Me and see!

"Therefore if any man be in Christ, he is a new creature: old things are passed away; behold, all things are become new" (2 Corinthians 5:17).

8

LIQUID LOVE

When they pierced My side liquid love poured out. The dark kingdom, the underworld, thought they had Me captive until they saw what poured out of My side and then they trembled! They remembered. They recognized the love. They remembered when My Father was their Father, too. Liquid love sparked that memory. A love that would give all for the one loved, that held back nothing – they trembled because they knew that in the face of such love they could not win.

"But one of the soldiers with a spear pierced his side, and forthwith came there out blood and water" (John 19:34).

"And when the centurion, which stood over against him, saw that he so cried out, and gave up the ghost, he said, Truly this man was the Son of God" (Mark 15:39).

ICHOR: According to ancient peoples the ethereal fluid in the veins of the ancient Greek gods was known as "Ichor" and took the place of blood. It was golden in colour. It looked like a mixture of blood and water and was said to be immortal. When the centurion saw the Blood mixed with water pouring out of Jesus' side after it had been pierced, it convinced him that Jesus was the Son of God. Water, or a fluid, mixed with His Blood would have given it a golden colour.

ALL CONQUERING LOVE

It was love, God's own heart that came out of the highest realm in Heaven. It was as though the stream of love that poured out of His Son's side came directly out of the heart of the Father. A poured out offering, a sweet libation, given out of the sweetness of a broken heart, a heart that had now gained the whole world and Whose Kingdom had invaded it.

Because of this liquid love with not one offence in it, having conquered the power of unforgiveness death could not hold Him. Christ released His Spirit into His Father's hands and He was free. The grave could not hold Him now because it had not one valid claim on Him. Death tried Him, searched Him out, saw the still body and cried out, "He is mine!" But as in the trying of the unblemished lambs by the priest, he found nothing. Even though Death examined Him to the marrow of His bones, he found no foothold, no place in which to put a flesh hook and drag Him down into the depths of the fiery, eternal grave in the regions of the underworld.

Death screamed in all his vileness because deep in the pit of his being he knew that he had been conquered and that because that doorway had now been opened there would be others that would go through it. He swirled in his madness, flying up into the air, a dark wind causing people to stumble as he swept past them. He felt the key of death sweep out of his hand as a Being of pure Light took it from him and he knew that he had no legal right to get it back. He was defeated — swept off his throne that he had cherished through the ages. There was only one hope now, as a master of deception, he had to encourage the human race to think that he still reigned.

Jesus, the Christ, the Anointed One of God, Son of the Most High, with the key of Death in His hand, descended down into the regions of Hell. The hordes of Hell could not hold Him, they could not touch Him; He was pure, overcoming Light. He had conquered every temptation, every desire, every thought and emotion, and He shone with a more brilliant intensity than they had ever seen. They recognized Him, this Son of God, they had lived with Him for eons until they had chosen to follow Lucifer, the shining one, and had believed all his shallow promises.

The brilliance of His Light overpowered them. They found dark corners in which to hide. Then they realised that He carried with Him the stigma of the cross and it was out of those wounds that the most brilliant of Lights was shining. But wait, there was another quality to those wounds and that Light, one unrecognizable as yet. They sought for the words to describe it, searched the spirit realm and then it came to them, the realisation, the word was, "Redemption."

With sinking hearts, they crawled even deeper into their holes, as they could see myriads of people slipping through their grasp, as they passed through a doorway of Light into the Kingdom of the Christ, the Anointed One. The keys of their regions of Hell slipped through their fingers, they could not hold on to them, every region was conquered, legally taken.

The Christ, the Anointed One, walked through the regions of Hell, delivering the captives, He held the keys of Death, Hell and the Grave.

"And now," He said, "It is truly finished!!"

Precious Lord,
Your love transcends the boundaries of earth
Reaching deeply into the realms of eternity
Boundless reality, taking form as liquid love,
Filling me, surrounding me
Until I transcend the limitations this earth imposes
Becoming eternal, clothed in love.

Rona Spiropoulos (2003)

"I am he that liveth, and was dead; and, behold, I am alive for evermore, Amen; and have the keys of hell and of death" (Revelation 1:18).

9

THE POWER OF AN ENDLESS LIFE

hen I said to Moses, "I AM that I AM," it was the most profound revelation in all of My Word. With those few words I opened up realms of understanding to him. He suddenly saw beyond the time and space that he lived in, into *eonia* time or eternal time where the eons of the past and the eons of the future passed before him. He saw realms of eternities past, universes and living beings. He saw creation coming together in the twinkling of an eye. He saw peoples and nations, wars, progress, the technical wonders of the age that you live in and he saw the end of it all and the eternities of the future. All it took was those few words to catapult him into a world of wonder beyond anything he had ever imagined. And, in all of it, I AM there! I AM at the center of it, I AM holding it all together and making it work, not through any divine strategies, but merely by My Presence. My settling in, My resting on My Throne in the Highest Heaven.

Eternity and the universes are Who I AM. Their working happens because I exist. I have always been, you cannot see it because it has not been given to you to see or understand. I would reveal it to you but you are not able to bear it now, you would misinterpret it or think it strange. My intense beauty would cause you to catapult into eternity. I have to show you shadows of Myself. The understanding of Who I AM has to come in moments, in shafts of enlightenment, in lightnings and thunderings that reveal My truth.

I have toned Myself down so that you could know Me, but even so, I still AM Who I AM, I lost nothing. I humbled Myself, I took on your form, I gave up the beauty of Who I AM to put on the earth clothes of human flesh. I AM the Word that became flesh for you and you read about My life that was faultless, without blemish, without those things that contradict love, but, I want to reveal to you the Power of My Endless Life so that I can take you up into My world and show you the mysteries of the universe. I want to show you all those things that I have in store for you; to show you how the universe works, how stars are formed and birthed, the timings that are so vital for the worlds to function, why orbits are circular in motion, the real reason behind the Tabernacle of My Presence and the celebration in Heaven when the veil of the Temple was rent.

The Power of the Endlessness of My Life is contained within My Blood, it imparts endlessness of Life as it is accessed and applied. It can never die, it can never clot and dry up because it was transmuted from the Blood in My earthly body into pure Light. When My Blood was in My human body, it had to conform to coursing through My veins and arteries. The vibration it gave out, the radiance of the Light that was its character, radiated out in a healing Light because you see My Life was in it. It has become transmuted and changed form because it only existed in a human body for a short time. Now it is omnipresent and omniscient and its eternal Light and Life are available to all. Press in to understand these things and I will give you understanding. Even when you don't understand, just trust Me, and accept it, and you will have available to you the Power of an Endless Life.

"And God said unto Moses, I AM THAT I AM: and he said, Thus shalt thou say unto the children of Israel, I AM hath sent me unto you" (Exodus 3:14).

"Who is made, not after the law of a carnal commandment, but after the power of an endless life" (Hebrews 7:16).

10

THE BLOOD IS A COVERING

*T*he Blood is a covering. When I hear your cry for help, I throw it over you like a mantle of Light, which lifts you up and out of your situation. It takes you into a realm of angelic protection. The angels respond to the Blood because even though they see it as Light it has a special quality to it. It was shed in love and has the quality of being able to buy a life in redemption. When My Blood covers a person bringing them into the New Birth, it is able to take sin and swallow it up into a place of non-existence, never to be thought of nor remembered again. It is able to pull the redeemed one through the "birth canal" of the Spirit and transform them and filter into them new life, My Life. It is the place of exchange.

So, when the angels see the Blood they recognise that that one is a citizen of their Kingdom and as such deserves the ambassadorial protection of a citizen living in another kingdom of which they are not a part. They understand what it means to be in the world but not of it. They realise the momentum of gradual transformation from glory to greater glory. The angels give respect to those that have been bought with the very precious Blood of their Lord and Master.

My Blood has buying power, it is a currency that is recognised in the world of the spirit. When My Blood buys a life, it is a transaction that cannot be denied by the under world. The life is bought and paid for in an exchange in which the rate never changes. It is the price of buying a lesser life with a greater life. I give My Life to buy yours and the transaction cannot be denied. The under world has no choice but to accept the transaction even though they cannot hold on to My Life because I already died and paid for you and they have no hold on Me. To them it is a great injustice but they know the laws and legalities of the spirit realm, they have no legal hold on Me, and when I buy you, their legal hold on you is broken, because you died with Me at Calvary.

There is a mystery in this; the Blood is able to take you through time to a pre-existing place and time, such as Calvary, locate you as a seed within My body on the cross and connect you with the generations of God, to bring you forth as a new creation with a new bloodline. Thus you become a chosen generation!

There are so many that have not made that connection yet. Intercede for them, bear in your body the fellowship of My sufferings for them and your reward will be seeing them gain their rewards when they stand before My Throne in a judgment of rewards.

My Blood will be celebrated throughout eternity when the Monuments of Grace, those bought by the Blood, are seen in Heaven and glory will be given to the Great Father of Lights and the Eternal Councils of Wisdom of the Godhead.

"And their sins and iniquities will I remember no more. Now where remission of these is, there is no more offering for sin" (Hebrew 10:17).

"Thou hast forgiven the iniquity of thy people, thou hast covered all their sin. Selah" (Psalm 85:2).

WHOM SHALL I SEND AND WHO WILL GO?

I knew the cost when I said I would go. The Living Creatures reacted, the angels turned their heads at the sound of My voice. There are some things spoken of in the Councils of Heaven that can be heard and there are some things that cannot. Heaven was included in this Council. They had seen the dilemma, they had watched Adam turn away from the glory and from His closeness to God and they wondered at it all.

They did not know the full plan, the most amazing, infinitely intricate plan of the ages, the redemption and the glorification of man to a higher degree. That which was lost would be restored by Me, and man would have access to higher regions than the Garden. Man would carry a greater Glory than Adam because everything in him would be brought into this Kingdom of Light by My Blood. Then he would be tested in every area to stretch him so that he could have the greatest capacity ever for My Glory.

You see, My Father and I, in agreement with the Holy Spirit, had a plan all along. Adam would be just a prototype, a test plan. There had to be those who would go beyond the innocence of childhood which had no choice, there had to be those that would have options and still choose Us. They had to be tempted and tried, they had to have all manner of paths laid before them, and gods laid before them, high positions and gods of Mammon laid before them and still choose Us. The temptations would prove to Whom they belonged. If they still loved Us and chose Us through it all, they would be counted worthy to carry greater glory and in carrying this greater glory they would become infused with it moment by moment. It is like putting a teabag into water, the strength of it gradually infuses through the water and it visibly changes and so does its taste.

We are talking about Sonship, the mature Sons who are able to rule and reign with Me. This is not something that is taken possession of by faith, but something that one becomes the closer one gets to the Father and by choosing Us above the honour of man. We have to know that you will go through trials and constraints and you will not turn away from Us. Sons are linked by Blood. They have acknowledged Whose they are and to deny Him would be to deny themselves.

The mystery is this, that in due time, they will become like Me, the Firstborn from the dead, I already passed through that way for them, if they will only believe.

"Thou madest him a little lower than the angels; thou crownedst him with glory and honour, and didst set him over the works of thy hands: Thou hast put all things in subjection under his feet. For in that he put all in subjection under him, he left nothing that is not put under him. But now we see not yet all things put under him. But we see Jesus, who was made a little lower than the angels for the suffering of death, crowned with glory and honour; that he by the grace of God should taste death for every man" (Hebrews 2:7-9).

12

ENOCH

"By faith Enoch was translated that he should not see death; and was not found, because God had translated him: for before his translation he had this testimony, that he pleased God" (Hebrews 11:5).

My son, Enoch, was not unique, he was a forerunner! If he was unique he would have entered a realm in the spirit where no one else could go. He is a forerunner because through his faith he accessed truths in Me, and, through his perfect trust, began to walk in them. As he walked his understanding opened up so that I could reveal to him greater truths. And so, he grew! Sometimes My truths have to bypass the complexity of your thinking and you cannot receive them because they are so simple.

Enoch pleased Me just because he believed Me. That is all it took! He trusted Me. Whatever I said, he accepted as truth and he never reviled My heart by wondering if there was something behind what I was saying, but took it at face-value. He had simplified his soul by becoming childlike. He trusted Me so much that he would step through the veil and visit with Me.

One day, I enjoyed his company so much that I did not want him to leave, so I took him and he "was not" on the other side of the veil, but he "is" on this side of the veil. His life was also bought by Me, but through his faith he dwelt in a realm of timelessness where I could die for him before I died on earth. He did not realise it, but by trusting Me even then, he had accessed the redemption of the "Lamb slain from the foundation of the world." My Blood cleansed him and covered him and enabled him to walk through the veil even though it had not yet been shed on the earth.

Timelessness is a mystery. But you will never understand it until you look beyond your everyday life and realise that there is a Kingdom within you that is ageless. Look within yourself to find the dwelling place of God, the Most Holy Place, the resting Place of the Most High, the Shekinah. Settle into that place, make yourself at home in it. Dwell there, worship out of that place, minister out of that place, live out of that place and your life and the lives of others will be transformed.

When you live there you have passed through the curtain of the Blood. You have been translated through your own soul and are living in the Most Holy Place where your spirit and My Holy Spirit have come into a union. That is the place of translation. When that Most Holy Place invades your whole being, you will walk with Me in perfect trust, in perfect union and it will be said of you, "She walked with God and she was not, because God took her."

13

EARTHLY PORTALS

*T*here are places in the earth where there has been intense spiritual activity. That activity has opened up gateways into realms of Heaven and realms in the heavenlies. These are realms of both Light and darkness according to the activity on the earth. Any person who has pressed in to know Me and has caused activity in the spirit realm, has facilitated a response from Me and Mine. When that response happens, doorways in the spirit, the realm of My Spirit and Kingdom, open up and provide a pathway for angels and living creatures to link earth with Heaven.

The height of the realm of the portal depends on how high the one causing the activity by pressing in is willing to go. If they are satisfied with a little then the portal will reach one of the lower levels of My Heaven. If they are never satisfied, nor comfortable, they will continue pressing in and reaching higher until they open up a portal into My Throne Room.

The degree of height of their portal will determine the rate and the abundance with which their prayers are answered. Never be satisfied so that you stop progressing. Never be satisfied nor stop pressing in. There are heights you never dreamed of and Throne

Rooms in abundance, for every different purpose. I am rich and without limitation; of My wealth and abundance there is no end. When I speak of wealth, I am speaking of knowledge and wisdom and the turning of the wheels of time in eternity, how to regulate the stars and their meanings. I have written My signs in the skies and not for the lower realms of mankind to know what will happen in their earthly dealings, that is designed to hold them earthbound and subject to a human spirit. I have written My signs so that the knowledge of Me can be studied out and clearly seen.

Portals access healing, they access deliverance, they access body parts, they access abundant supply and much more. They access the riches of My Kingdom which when accessed with a pure heart are not subject to the god of Mammon. There are those that access wealth through portals into lower regions but this wealth does not have the ability to multiply when given away. They have tapped in to the wealth of the god of Mammon. They are self-made.

Portals provide a stairway for My angels to go back and forth from earth to Heaven and from Heaven to earth. Where there is a portal there is no resistance in the Spirit – My Spirit and the Heavenly beings can work freely. They feel a warm welcome when they come down to minister and so they go back and forth quite happily. That place on earth is filled with My Presence so they feel at home.

There are places on the earth where there has been great devotion and purity of heart with brokenness before Me, places where there has been high worship in Spirit and truth. Those places have become portals of access that have been established on the earth and are jealously guarded by My angels. Great warrior angels are in those places because I have allowed a unique richness of My Presence to dwell there. They are notable places on the earth that are available to all but the casual observer. They are places of My habitation, My Shekinah, where I come to commune with My people.

14

THE SHEKINAH GLORY

Where is the place of My rest and where is the place of My habitation?

The Shekinah is the settling in of My glory. It is My glory come down to rest and take up habitation. It is a holy habitation where only I dwell and I do not share My dwelling place with another. It is the cloud of My Presence out of which I speak. When My Shekinah is there sometimes you might hear Me speak to your spirit man and give you direction. I will tell you of things to come, of realms of greater glory, of secrets and mysteries of My Kingdom and how these mysteries can be accessed and used to further My Kingdom. If your heart is pure and fully focused on My will, I will come down and make My habitation with you and speak to you face to face.

You have read that no man can see God and live, but I tell you this; that as the Blood covers you, I see My Son and I see captured within you everything that you were meant to be. You cannot help but become who you really are as I come down to make My resting place with you.

You are My pride and joy, the blood-bought ones! The ones to whom I can make myself manifest and dwell with, the ones to whom I can give the mantle of My glory. It will rest upon them for they will govern on the earth with that mantle, it will be their Tent of Meeting, their place of communion with Me as they take Me to the ends of the earth.

Covet nothing but My manifested Presence dwelling with you, being a part of all you do, for within it is every delight and every abundance and pure joy. Out of it will flow the river of My love and every provision that My people need. I will reveal myself for Who I AM and the people will cry, "Holy, holy, holy! The High and Holy One has visited us and we are not consumed!" They will understand what has always been on My heart, that they have a place within Me that is just for them. When My people see My resting Presence they will want to know Me and will realise Who I AM.

The scales of religion and the teachings of religion will fall off their hearts and they will see with the knowledge of intimacy that My great desire is for each one of them and to meet and fellowship with them. My people will realise that through the Blood of My Son they have entry into My Shekinah and I will catch them up and love them and they will cry out with the joy of knowing Me and I will open My heart and they will see Me and talk to Me face to face.

Establish places for Me on the earth, places where I may come down and find a resting place for My glory.

"And thou shalt put the mercy seat above upon the ark; and in the ark thou shalt put the testimony that I shall give thee. And there I will meet with thee, and I will commune with thee from above the mercy seat, from between the two cherubims which are upon the ark of the testimony, of all things which I will give thee in commandment unto the children of Israel" (Exodus 25:21-22).

15

A PILLAR OF FIRE

When you see a pillar of fire in your home or in your church you will know that a time of refining has come. But, do not fear because I have prayed for you. My refining is more to be desired than fine gold. My refining is the most valuable asset on earth because it prepares you for greatness. It prepares you to live a refined life, it has nothing to do with manners or etiquette, although these will be a by-product, but it has everything to do with your station or ranking in the Spirit. Don't despise My refining and think that I have turned away from you. Don't you remember the Scripture, which says that those whom I love I chasten so that they can be sons? (Hebrew 12:5-8) Refining develops grace and purity so that you can walk in the midst of My pillar of fire and it can go where you go.

There are pillars of fire in My courts. They are the seven spirits of My Holy Spirit, they are spirits of ascension glory, they stand guarding the way into My highest courts. Only one who has walked through intense fire and never left My side can walk in these realms and receive from these realms. These are hidden realms, which no one can enter except by invitation. That realm is guarded by My burning ones, the Seraphim.

This is the realm of the Stones of Fire, the Stones which speak in a language only a few, even in Heaven, can understand, because they speak mysteries through worship. They expose all things hidden. It was the whisperings and the murmurings of the Stones of Fire that exposed Lucifer's shadow of turning. It was the discomfort and intensity of the Stones of Fire that told him he no longer belonged there because he had changed.

Welcome the intensity of the Pillar of Fire, it shows that My Presence has come and is preparing you and preparing the place where you are for a greater glory. Sometimes you won't see it, you will only feel as though you have encountered something so holy, so pure that it has left you physically shaken. This is the beginning! Embrace it, because it is for your good, your eternity depends on it. The degree of your refining will determine the place that you stand in for all eternity. High, high callings require high, high refinings.

Walk with Me amongst the Stones of Fire. Meet Me in this place!

I will wait for you as you allow the Pillar of Fire to do its work and then we will have the joy of unhindered communion.

"And ye have forgotten the exhortation which speaketh unto you as unto children, My son, despise not thou the chastening of the Lord, nor faint when thou art rebuked of him: For whom the Lord loveth he chasteneth, and scourgeth every son whom he receiveth. If ye endure chastening, God dealeth with you as with sons; for what son is he whom the father chasteneth not? But if ye be without chastisement, whereof all are partakers, then are ye bastards, and not sons" (Hebrews 12:5-8).

When He has tried me, I'll come forth as gold
The fires of affliction will not mar my soul.
I know that God loves me, my life has a goal,
And when He has tried me, I'll come forth as gold.

Gwen R. Shaw (1995)

16

STAND FAST – IMMOVABLE IN ME!

"Who hath delivered us from the power of darkness, and hath translated us into the kingdom of his dear Son" (Colossians 1:13).

Be assured that you have been translated out of darkness into everlasting Light, for you have been translated into Me. I in you and you in Me, an everlasting union. When you stand in Me, you stand as Me. Wherever you go you stand as Me. All that I am stands with you because as you have My Blood you have My Life. This is not just a theory, it is a Life living itself out in you in resurrection power. You were crucified with Me and therefore you have been raised up in resurrection with Me too. There is no argument or plea in this case. The verdict has been reached – it is finished!

Just walk it out. "As He is so are we in this world" (1 John 4:17). These words say it very clearly, you are as Me. The perfection of who you are is already established in you. Love is perfected in you – just walk it out. You seek Me for what you already have – walk in it! Stand immovable, as Christ on the earth. Do what I did. Preach the good news to the poor in spirit those ready to accept Me, and if you are rejected, once again, you stand as Me, for I was rejected, too!

This I say again, you are already made perfect because you died with Me and rose up when I did. As you rose up with Me all the limitations of the natural man fell off you. You have become limitless. Do not limit yourself. You have a life that is abundant in its fullness! Live like you believe it to be truly so.

What can separate you from Me? We are one, you just have to know it and believe it. There is a love connection between us, covenant love that cannot be broken.

Ah, I see your desire for Me, but I am giving you a challenge, let your desire match Mine, let your passion for Me match Mine for you. Then we will be evenly matched, equally yoked, I will have a Bride that is fully matured and not one that is still in her puppy love stage. Where I go she will follow and not follow begging something of Me, she trusts and knows that I am the source of every supply and that I give liberally.

Be steadfast and surefooted, I will see that your foot does not slide. Go beyond hope, and trust. Trust knows, it does not just hope, it knows and is confident that I am Who I say I am. I am yours and you are Mine. Intertwined in love, intertwined in divine union, the mystery of marriage. The lesser surrendering to the Greater, the Greater giving all to the lesser, intertwined by a cord of eternity because you came out of Me and I created you for My divine plan. Walk it out!

"I am crucified with Christ: nevertheless I live; yet not I, but Christ liveth in me: and the life which I now live in the flesh I live by the faith of the Son of God, who loved me, and gave himself for me" (Galatians 2:20).

"Even when we were dead in sins, hath quickened us together with Christ, (by grace ye are saved;) And hath raised us up together, and made us sit together in heavenly places in Christ Jesus" (Ephesians 2:5-6).

A SACRED PLACE OF HONOUR

There is a sacred place in the Heavens where My Blood is kept, from there it is released onto the earth when it is called for. It is a treasure, it is regarded with deep respect because its power is known by the Heavenly inhabitants.

It is in an area set apart for honour. It is similar to places of great honour on the earth where men and women are honoured for their great achievements or their great valour, but it is of much greater beauty. It is kept in a circular open portico with exquisitely marbled columns At the top of each burns an open flame. The Blood is kept in a big, shallow, golden chalice on a pedestal made of molten gold, which moves within its form and murmurs honour to that which it maintains. There are mighty hosts that surround it, that are like a wall of fire, they stand like sentinels, quietly giving honour.

My Blood, as it lies in the chalice, does not look like blood would on earth, but it looks like a vibrant cloud of incandescent light, and it continually speaks to Me of mercy. In the mystery of Heavenly things I am still in My Blood and it still is a part of Me, so it speaks what is in My heart.

When you look at situations and people, look through a wall of My Blood, your attitude will change to one of mercy. You see, even in My judgments, I remember mercy. It is like a sweet oil, a fragrance that pervades the atmosphere and changes hearts and situations.

William Shakespeare tapped into a divine truth when he wrote the following words in his play, "The Merchant of Venice":

"The quality of mercy is not strain'd,
  It droppeth as the gentle rain from heaven
  Upon the place beneath: it is twice blest;
  It blesseth him that gives and him that takes:
  'Tis mightiest in the mightiest: it becomes
  The throned monarch better than his crown;
  His sceptre shows the force of temporal power,
  The attribute to awe and majesty,
  Wherein doth sit the dread and fear of kings;
  But mercy is above this sceptred sway;
  It is enthroned in the hearts of kings,
  It is an attribute to God himself;
  And earthly power doth then show likest God's
  When mercy seasons justice. Therefore, Jew,
  Though justice be thy plea, consider this,
  That, in the course of justice, none of us
  Should see salvation: we do pray for mercy;
  And that same prayer doth teach us all to render
  The deeds of mercy."

As Portia, a brilliant young woman, spoke these words in the trial of the Merchant of Venice, she saw beyond earthly justice and saw the Heart of God, Who wishes to judge no man. Judgment is not His predisposition, "the Law" is not His divine order. Judgment comes when the Laws of Grace and Mercy are consistently violated.

Mercy cries loudest when the deeds are foulest, until mercy can no longer prevail and the wheels of consequence begin to turn.

But, the cry of mercy vibrates through the Heavens, because it is spoken through My Blood. When the councils of Heaven meet to determine events on earth, the Blood speaks. It is a reminder to a long-suffering God, it is a reminder to the Justice-Keepers in Heaven.

Sometimes mercy means that a life has to be taken to spare other lives. Sometimes a destiny has to be lost to spare the destiny of others.

Mercy has a profound quality when it is combined with godly Wisdom. Who can hold the scales of justice? It requires a steady hand and a merciful heart, but those scales in Heaven, have within themselves the pattern for judgment and mercy, and are instilled with the wisdom that comes from the Godhead.

In your intercessions for a nation, remember mercy, in your prayers for one who struggles or is lost, remember mercy. It is a sound that speaks with the same voice that My Blood speaks. A Voice greater than that of Abel, greater than a voice crying out for vengeance, "In Your wrath, Father, remember mercy."

"The quality of mercy is not strained…," it has an ebb and flow, like the tides of the sea, but it reigns supreme, like a King holding out his scepter to his wife and Queen, Esther.

It was mercy that saved a nation on that day.

"O LORD, I have heard thy speech, and was afraid: O LORD, revive thy work in the midst of the years, in the midst of the years make known; in wrath remember mercy" (Habakkuk 3:2).

"Blessed are the merciful for they shall obtain mercy" (Matthew 5:7).

18

THE VAULTS OF HEAVEN

I will open the vaults of Heaven to all who seek to know My heart and let them in, so that they can see the treasures that are kept there. Every noble deed is kept there, every tear, every drop of blood shed by My martyrs they are treasures. The things that humanity walks over, I treasure. Tears are kept in bottles, each one of them a gem. I use them to wash situations clean because they flow out of a broken heart, and ultimately, they are a part of the healing stream that flows from My Father's Throne.

Noble deeds are recorded so that they will not be forgotten because they are a first fruits of greatness on the earth. They open up a gateway of valour and nobility that others can go through. Deeds of lives being laid down for another and of those that love not their lives unto death, those that have given their lives wholly to Me. Great lovers! Those who have done exploits for love, those who have lived exemplary lives. They are all recorded here.

Another area has records and trophies of those who are Heroes of the Faith. Those that have refused to allow the curtains of Heaven to be shut to them and have broken through realms of glory and realms of the supernatural. Here are those that would not live ordinary lives, they refused the mundane and the mediocre, and stepped into a world beyond the ordinary. Here are those that went beyond time into future realms and lived in them; for them eternity was in the moment they were living in. They shattered kingdoms with their words, believing that I spoke through them. They opened up the supernatural to those that would listen. Believe them and follow their example. They are My Bandoliers in whom I placed My ammunition so that they can change a world!

In another area of the vault are unclaimed promises, promises that have been held in safekeeping, waiting to be accessed. It is true that My Word never returns to Me void, but these "Words" have never been sent out to see what they would accomplish. They are Powerhouses, waiting here in this vault, waiting to be claimed. Precious promises of latent power that could radically change lives.

In this final area that I want to show you are the destinies of lives that have been cut short. Aborted babies that were never given the chance to choose to live their lives for Me and children that died because of abuse. If My people would only rise up and call on My Blood to cover this bloodshed of the innocent, if they would only call on My Blood to bring conviction to the perpetrators, My angels would be alerted to work and My Blood would be as the Hound of Heaven, chasing them until they could no longer stand their guilt and fall on their faces crying out for mercy! When will My people learn to stand in their full authority and decree the end of this merciless practice in a civilized society?

Pray for My people to rise to the challenge of who I call them to be in this age! Pray for them to be strong and courageous and neither stumble nor be afraid for I AM WITH THEM!

19

WORSHIP MAKES THE WORLD GO AROUND

*I*t is not money, but worship, that makes the world go around. Worship keeps the planets in orbit, it is the momentum through which the universe works. It is the power that is released to My angels and is the energy that surrounds My Throne. I have need of nothing to sustain Me, but I have chosen to include you in the workings of My universe and in the activities of the angels and the Heavenly beings.

Worship is not just a nice feeling, it is not just a time to release pent-up emotions, it is not about choosing to be expressive or not be expressive. Worship is an energy that rises up and creates and inspires and clears up atmospheres. The extent to which worship is expressed is the degree to which this happens. It also depends on whether or not the worshippers put into their worship their whole heart, soul, mind and strength.

Your worship may only clear up the atmosphere around you and bring yourself under the authority of the Holy Spirit OR you may clear up the atmosphere of your group, OR your county, OR your city OR your nation. But, when you worship with all that you are and everything that you have, your worship can affect your whole solar system in ways that you cannot know now.

Worship brings order out of disorder. Planets that have gone off kilter are lined up through worship. It is the atmosphere of Heaven released into the cosmos and the atmosphere of Heaven brings order. It is so simple.

In the midst of your situations, when you worship you are bringing the order of Heaven into them. When disorder affects you, when discouragement and dismay trouble you – worship! When an attack is launched against you – worship! When prayer seems unanswered – worship! It will all come back into order, because the atmosphere is being changed by the energy released out of your worship.

There is a *dunamis* authority released out of worship, which is why those that have the highest authority in My Kingdom are great worshippers. David was a relentless worshipper and I placed on him kingly authority. It was his as he pushed through every boundary and determined to worship me. He accessed it and then I anointed him with this kingly authority on earth, but, it was already done in the Heavenlies.

When you open your heart up to Me to release pure worship, your heart is stretched and the Most Holy Place within you becomes enlarged and reaches out beyond yourself until it captures atmospheres. Don't think that because you can't see it nothing is happening while you are worshipping. There are great gains taking place and you and I are entering into a relationship of mutual admiration.

Worship Me, take territory, and let's enjoy each other in the process!

"And they rose early in the morning, and went forth into the wilderness of Tekoa: and as they went forth, Jehoshaphat stood and said, Hear me, O Judah, and ye inhabitants of Jerusalem; Believe in the LORD your God, so shall ye be established; believe his prophets, so shall ye prosper. And when he had consulted with the people, he appointed singers unto the LORD, and that should praise the beauty of holiness, as they went out before the army, and to say, Praise the LORD; for his mercy endureth for ever. And when they began to sing and to praise, the LORD set ambushments against the children of Ammon, Moab, and mount Seir, which were come against Judah; and they were smitten. For the children of Ammon and Moab stood up against the inhabitants of mount Seir, utterly to slay and destroy them: and when they had made an end of the inhabitants of Seir, every one helped to destroy another. And when Judah came toward the watch tower in the wilderness, they looked unto the multitude, and, behold, they were dead bodies fallen to the earth, and none escaped.

And when Jehoshaphat and his people came to take away the spoil of them, they found among them in abundance both riches with the dead bodies, and precious jewels, which they stripped off for themselves, more than they could carry away: and they were three days in gathering of the spoil, it was so much. And on the fourth day they assembled themselves in the valley of Berachah; for there they blessed the LORD: therefore the name of the same place was called, The valley of Berachah, unto this day. Then they returned, every man of Judah and Jerusalem, and

Jehoshaphat in the forefront of them, to go again to Jerusalem with joy; for the LORD had made them to rejoice over their enemies. And they came to Jerusalem with psalteries and harps and trumpets unto the house of the LORD. And the fear of God was on all the kingdoms of those countries, when they had heard that the LORD fought against the enemies of Israel. So the realm of Jehoshaphat was quiet: for his God gave him rest round about" (2 Chronicles 20:20-30).

20

A Pathway through Your Hearts

The electrical impulses that run through your hearts are a picture of My own. I don't need anything to sustain My Heartbeat. I don't need an electric charge to keep My heart beating. It is the electrical charge that came out of My heart, when I loved you before I even created you, that I breathed into man, that still keeps your hearts beating. You were ignited when you were in Adam's loins.

Your hearts were ignited for greatness, for overcoming. The electrical charge to your heart enables you to connect with eternity because My breath that I breathed has never stopped giving life. It is as life-giving now as it was when I breathed into Adam at creation.

But, you were chosen for greatness, this generation is the transitional generation that lives in times of trouble on the earth, but the reality of the resurrection power of the Christ, and the glory of His reign is only a veil away. You can choose which side of the veil you want to live on, but your hearts have been charged with resurrection power through the power of His Blood mingling with yours.

Think about it! Do you really want to remain in the power of this age, or do you want to live in the power of the age of overcoming which is, at this time, only a breath away. Your hearts are charged and ready for it if you will only acknowledge it and receive it. You can be given a gift, but it is only yours if you receive it.

Press through to discover a new realm of living where you rule and reign with Christ even as your feet still stand on this earth. You can have ruling authority because of a pathway cut through your hearts for the King of Glory to come marching through. This is also known as circumcision of the heart. You will be forever changed because two people cannot live in the same heart. Divine union comes when one surrenders to another, or prefers another because that one has entered into a season of love that will never pass.

Two hearts beating as one, two minds thinking as one and I remind you that I can never think like you do, one of us will have to give up their life. Calvary has already happened and you died there with Me; ask Me to make that a reality for you. Once you acknowledge that reality by faith, you are set free to live forevermore in the power of the resurrected Christ.

Let the vibrancy of your life be your love for Me.

Taste and see that I am good! I am like the most fragrant anointing oil and the sweetest of honey.

And…My joy…is to be with you!

"Having therefore, brethren, boldness to enter into the holiest by the blood of Jesus, By a new and living way, which he hath consecrated for us, through the veil, that is to say, his flesh; And

having an high priest over the house of God; Let us draw near with a true heart in full assurance of faith, having our hearts sprinkled from an evil conscience, and our bodies washed with pure water" (Hebrews 10:19-22).

"I am crucified with Christ: nevertheless I live; yet not I, but Christ liveth in me: and the life which I now live in the flesh I live by the faith of the Son of God, who loved me, and gave himself for me" (Galatians 2:20).

"Thy lips, O my spouse, drop as the honeycomb: honey and milk are under thy tongue; and the smell of thy garments is like the smell of Lebanon" (Song of Solomon 4:11).

PURE LIGHT

He dwells in regions of light. *"He covers Himself with light as a garment"* (Psalm 104:2).

The intensity of the Light that I dwell in goes beyond anything known in earthly realms. Even My light, which comes out of servants, does not have the same intensity. Those that walk closely with Me do have light radiating out of them, but that is toned down intensity. My light that I dwell in is so intense that any darkness cannot live in it, it is swallowed up and ceases to exist. If I allowed the intensity of My light on earth, every dark thing would be pulled into it and cease to exist. There would be mass destruction on the earth and even My own people would cease to exist.

This would not be judgment, it is the way of the highest Heaven. The laws of these regions are the laws of intense light. Light is the measure! It is the plumbline! Everything in these high regions work according to whether they can stand in the intensity of My light, which is Who I am. If it cannot stand in the same intensity it does not happen. That is why not everyone is permitted into the Throne room even of those that have already come into Heaven. They have to go through the purification process and gradually enter into greater regions of light.

69

The way you live on earth should not be whether something is right or wrong, that measure is for the unredeemed. The measure of the way you live on earth should be, does it conform to My light. The more that you live in this way the more you are transformed and the Light of My Presence lives in you. The more you are transformed the greater the intensity of the light that is able to dwell in you.

Use your time with Me to bring expansion of your inner regions, surrender every fortress, open yourself to the invasion of My Spirit Who comes with My light. Yes, it will cause you discomfort in the natural realm to live like this but your surroundings will be transformed by My light that is in you. The discomfort comes because you will live in a different intensity and being in surroundings of lesser intensity causes discomfort. Only My love can cover these situations and that is available to you.

I surround Myself with light, rainbows of colour. In the atmosphere of the highest Heaven, light is not contained the way it is on earth, but has the freedom to prism out into a magnitude of colours, flaring out into great displays of glory. It is similar to a fanfare on earth and it lets the inhabitants in My Kingdom know that the King is in His courts, on His Throne, ruling and reigning. These flares of glory can be seen throughout Heaven even in the lower regions because they are signs of My ruling Presence. In the lower regions of Heaven they are diffused because those that live in that realm are not used to high intensity so I have to gradually introduce them to the glory.

"In him was life; and the life was the light of men. And the light shineth in darkness; and the darkness comprehended it not. There was a man sent from God, whose name was John" (John 1:4-6).

22

THE GIFT OF TONGUES

"And when the day of Pentecost was fully come, they were all with one accord in one place. And suddenly there came a sound from heaven as of a rushing mighty wind, and it filled all the house where they were sitting. And there appeared unto them cloven tongues like as of fire, and it sat upon each of them. And they were all filled with the Holy Ghost, and began to speak with other tongues, as the Spirit gave them utterance" (Acts 2:1-4).

The Gift of Tongues as spoken about in My Word is a misunderstood and neglected gift. It is a gift that I give to My Blood-bought ones and that gift is made manifest when My Spirit covers the tongue like a sheath of light. As that one speaks, moves their tongue and produces sounds, the tongue through the Blood of Christ becomes multi-dimensional entering into the dimensions of the Spirit in which that person dwells and ever pressing into dimensions beyond.

Your tongue is a rudder! It will take you where you want to go, but it will also take you where you say it will. Pray in tongues as often as you can so that you become multi-dimensional. Let the Holy Spirit provide the covering for your tongue and take it into My

71

courts and speak to Me about the matters of earth because He and I and the Blood agree together in a Divine Council.

Sometimes you wonder what are those sounds coming out of you, they are higher than you, that is why you do not understand them now. I have to go beyond your mind and even your godly wisdom, because the Holy Spirit could be praying about earthly situations but He could also be praying about the mysteries of Heaven and the timings of their release upon the earth.

When you pray in tongues, see your tongue covered in a sheath of light and extending out of you into My dimensions because that is exactly what is happening. As you dip your tongue into Heaven you carry back on it what I desire to release to the earth, whether answers to prayer or the Mysteries of the Kingdom.

The tongue is a powerful weapon because it has breakthrough power, it can break bones or it can break into dimensions. But, I, in My divine wisdom and counsel, have covered it with the Blood of Christ to preserve it for Myself and to give it an eternal quality so that it can speak of eternal things and the Voice in the Blood will use your tongue to speak of mercy and righteousness. My Spirit, Who always works in agreement with Me, uses it to bring about powerful movements in the Spirit. The greatness of His strategy is that the words spoken in tongues stay very high above the radar of the Enemy.

The Enemy and your own mind cannot interfere with these plans. They are the hidden strategies of My Spirit and they always bring about My desired end.

"For he that speaketh in an unknown tongue speaketh not unto men, but unto God: for no man understandeth him; howbeit in the spirit he speaketh mysteries" (1 Corinthians 14:2).

23

THE SECRET OF GREATNESS

here is a secret to My greatness. It is not the power of the Throne from which I rule. It is not just because I need nothing to sustain My life. It is not because I have authority over the whole universe and can order the events of earth. It is not because I am omnipresent and omniscient, because by My Word I create. It is not because I, in My Councils, ordained the greatest plan the universe has ever known, the plan of the redemption of man. It is not because everything around Me is life-giving, nothing can remain around Me and not be infused with abundance of life.

I will tell you what it is. It is because within My love I have the Power of Release. I do not command adoration, I do not command nor demand that I am worshipped and held in high esteem. I release My people to choose where they will stand and how they will come to Me. I would prefer complete surrender because by it they enter into abundant life and into the fullness of My purpose for their lives, but I don't demand it. That is the difference between Me and the gods of the heathen.

I knew, in the Garden of Eden, what direction Adam would take and the consequences for mankind and the consequences for

My Son. He had already been slain and His Blood made available in the mysterious foreknowledge and blendings of time in Heaven's dimensions. Even though I knew, I did not interfere with Adam's free will. I gave him the parameters that would keep him in fellowship with Me and then I released him.

Greatness releases; releases people to be themselves, to become what I intend for them to be, to have the joy of serving Me freely without oppression. I have the power to control every working of the universe and all the workings of man, but instead I ordain events and many of these things are subject to the free will of man. I even leave him free to enter into the consequences of doing what is wrong.

When you love, add the Power of Release to your love, when you pray, add the Power of Release to your prayers and as you live your life for Me, release Me to work according to My will by always saying, *"…nevertheless, Thy will be done."* Let this not only be your prayer, but let it be your attitude.

If you learn this you will have learned a great lesson. Release allows the seed of destiny to open up and grow into a mighty tree, which will provide shade for others and will produce a multiplication of seeds of the same kind.

Trust Me enough to take your hands off situations and people and see what I will do!

"Saying, Father, if thou be willing, remove this cup from me: nevertheless not my will, but thine, be done" (Luke 22:42).

24

THE LIGHT AND THE GLORY

My light gives you enlightenment and revelation. It opens up the eyes of your spirit so that you can look through the dimensions and see My glory. Your eyes are like gateways, which open up to receive and to give. When you see the glory of My Throne Room, it is taken in by you into your spirit. That is why you must prepare within your spirit a platform or dwelling to sustain My glory, or else the experience will not last. You prepare this place through hunger for Me and for My glory. The greater your hunger, the greater will be your capacity for the glory.

Your hunger is like light being sent out from you and I see it from My high Heavenly place and I am alerted to you. Nothing moves Me like hunger. It is like a mother that hears the cry of her hungry baby – it causes a response! Your hunger fills Me with joy and I get up and begin to swirl and as I swirl I release glory to you. Don't ever let your hunger die or lose its intensity, if you do, you will lose momentum in the Spirit.

Let My enlightenment, the light of the revelation of Who I am, fill you with a passion to know Me. I wait for you to stand before Me in the fullness of maturity so that I can adorn you with garments of light, so that you can be like Me. You are hungry for a place in Me that your spirit knows exists even though in your mind you are unaware of it. It is a position in My Courts where you can stand as a pillar, a sentinel and a watcher, utterly consecrated to Me. Watching where My eyes watch and feeling every movement of My expressions and My thoughts so that when we look at each other we can speak without words.

That place is waiting for you, just turn your gaze to Me. In those moments of "beholding" Me you begin to know Me and you will find that I am everything your heart has ever desired. My Bride, My Sister, My Spouse, come and visit My Courts regularly until the atmosphere of Heaven pervades your being and you become a carrier of My glory. Position yourself, by obeying the leading of the Holy Spirit and you will find My Courts always open to you.

Enter into a place of rest where there is no struggle. My Holy Spirit will anoint you with anointing oils to prepare you for your task, your position. In the Spirit realm that place is kept for you alone. Only your feet can fill those shoes. That is how My Kingdom works, I have ordained purposes for each one and only they can do it best. Their place remains vacant until they fill it and I will do all that I can to draw them into the depth of consecration needed to fulfill their destiny.

Let your hunger draw you into My Courts and into the fullness of all that is destined just for you.

"Blessed are they which do hunger and thirst after righteousness: for they shall be filled" (Matthew 5:6).

"I sleep, but my heart waketh: it is the voice of my beloved that knocketh, saying, Open to me, my sister, my love, my dove, my undefiled: for my head is filled with dew, and my locks with the drops of the night" (Song of Solomon 5:2).

25

CROWNS, GARMENTS AND MANTLES

*P*icture this scene: My Son dressed in royal garments, a crown of the most glorious jewels on His head, radiating lights. The wounds from the crown of thorns that was placed on His head are portals out of which the glory of His Being now radiates. Dropping from His shoulders is a Blood-red mantle with a train, it is edged with what looks like white ermine. His garments are white with the lights of the rainbow in them. He is resplendent in majesty. He walks down the aisle to Our Throne like a ruling Monarch, which He is, together with Me. Heaven is entranced with His beauty. He is pure Light mingled with Love and vibrancy of Life.

If He would reveal Himself as this Christ on earth, the whole world would be drawn to Him, some would bow the knee only because they had to. He is irresistible when He reveals Himself for Who He is. But, We have chosen the foolishness of preaching that all may choose through their own free will.

Heaven is filled with beautiful garments, crowns and mantles. The Blood-bought ones will wear them here, not because you need to cover your nakedness but because they are part of the beauty of My Kingdom. Some crowns are made up of a single huge gem, but the gems here are not like the ones on earth, these have life, and the radiance and the colours they give off tell a story. There are some crowns that are very unique in their design because they were earned in unusual circumstances, but they all tell their own tale.

Mantles are more extravagant than anything seen on earth even from the highest fashion houses. Some are jewel-encrusted, some look similar to exquisite fabrics on the earth but have a vibrancy that only Heaven can give. They, like the crowns, are part of the wearer's life and have tales to tell.

Heaven's garments are beautiful in their richness of colour, elaborate in their embroidery and ornamentation and are regal because everyone here has had their dignity restored to them. They differ in how elaborate they are, but even the simplest has Heaven's beauty. There are colours and fabrics and designs all perfectly suited to one's personality and calling and stature in Christ. Keep forever reaching higher, to live a higher life, attaining everything that was bought and paid for by the Living Christ for you. Begin to see yourself with the adornings of Heaven and you will recognise the degree of love I have for My people and how I long for them to see themselves already in the garments that I have prepared for them.

The spirit world recognizes the garments that you wear even now, because they speak about your life, your destiny and what you have obtained in the Spirit. Every level and every dimension requires a change of garment, they have all been prepared and are just waiting for My people to come up higher.

"He maketh my feet like hinds' feet: and setteth me upon my high places" (2 Samuel 22:34).

26

MY INCANDESCENT LOVE

My love for My people is like an incandescent flame burning in My heart. It was the power of this flame that brought about the Plan of the Ages, the Redemption of Man. Even as I let you go, My heart was aflame with love and longing for you. When you walked away I did not take My eyes off you. I knew that as long as your entire life was lived in the natural realm we could never enjoy each other. The only way that I could draw you back was to open up a place for you in the realm of the spirit where you could have entrance into My world and we could meet and walk again in the cool of the evening.

The same flame burns in the heart of My Son and in My Holy Spirit, you see, We are not only love, We are burning love. We know no moderation in love, We can only love passionately because to love any other way would be to deny Who We are.

We have drawn you so close, through the Blood of My Son, that We live in you and you live in Us. We would have it no other way. We enjoy your presence even more than you enjoy Ours. I know this is hard for you to believe because your senses are not as finely tuned as Ours. I am acutely sensitive, I feel every shadow of turning when your focus is even slightly off Me. It does not affect My realm, but I feel it and it does affect you because you miss the whisperings that I put into your spirit. Practice being as single-eyed as the dove, so that your eyes are always filled with Me and your focus is fully on Me.

Come, My Beloved, let's agree together and walk together and you will find times of refreshing in My Presence. I will talk to you about things that you want to know. I will take you and show you the wonders of creation, how worlds and universes were formed as I breathed out the Words of Creation. I will give you insight into the Plan of the Ages and My plans for the age that you are living in.

These are transitional days, days like no other, and every day needs to be fresh and new for you, because as changes are taking place on the earth, your thinking has to be renewed daily. You cannot live with the opinions and thoughts of yesterday because they only worked for yesterday. Even as you see things happen on earth that are following a pattern of yesterday, remember that I am ahead of earth time. I live in your future and if you are to be a prophet on the earth you need to live in the future and bring it into your present so that your present becomes an eternal moment.

Heaven is not taken by surprise by what is happening on the earth. There is a momentum now in Heaven that is increasing because, as the enemy is working out his strategies, the strategies of Heaven are already in place. I am ahead of him. Speak out My Words and My strategies for these times as I give them to you and they will be established upon the earth and rejoice that you have been chosen to live in these days.

These are the days of regeneration, days when you will begin to understand the true meaning of being of a new bloodline. Ask Me about it, and learn about it before events on earth pressure you into learning about it. If you stay ahead you can be at rest!

27

COME AND SEE
THE STARS WITH ME

*T*he Heavens declare My glory! I decorate the Heavens with My stars, in the midst of trouble on the earth you can look up and see the stars and know that I am there, regulating the universe. When I showed Abraham the stars and told him that his descendents would be like them, he did not realise that the stars were not a fixed number. He did realise that they, could not be numbered by man, but he did not realise that there are stars born every day just like His descendents.

When I put the stars and the planets in the heavens with their sun and their moons I put them in a particular orbit, which caused a magnetic pull on each other that would keep them within their own solar system. Man is still discovering the wonder of this. Although they have made many discoveries, they have not discovered the unknown factor, which keeps all things together. If they read the Scriptures they would know that My Son sustains all things with the Word of His power.

When He chose to redeem the world He became the Heir of all things because even though He was Co-Creator, through the fall of Lucifer, there were stations in the heavens that were closed and kept captive by the angels of the underworld. Those had to be bought back by One that had willingly passed through the valley of the shadow of death and had come out on the other side in resurrection life. It took Blood to redeem those worlds.

That is why I want to show them to you and to all that delight in seeing these things. I want to show off the trophies of redemption bought by My Son. He is My delight! When I look at Him and see the glory of His majesty, I want all the world to know Him and I, through My Holy Spirit. Begin to stir up the hearts of My people to pray, pray, pray for those that are yet unsaved.

One day, the world is going to look up at the brightness of His appearing and many will lose their minds when they see His beauty and feel the pull of His love defying gravity, because the darkness within them will keep them earthbound. In an instant they will understand that all their lives they have served the wrong god!

Pray, pray, pray! While there is still time. My will is that all be saved. There are those that will choose their own way, but, He will not lose one of those that I have given Him!

"...And I come to thee. Holy Father, keep through thine own name those whom thou hast given me, that they may be one, as we are" (John 17:11b).

28

A LAMB IN ALL HIS GENTLENESS

I stand and watch, captivated! I see a Lamb in all His gentleness, lying, a river of Blood pouring out of His side. I want to help Him, but, a hand holds me back. My child, says the Father, you cannot now understand, these are the mysteries of My Kingdom. I had to wound Him and I had to wound Him with joy because out of that wound will flow myriads of peoples and nations. You see, the Lamb is but a seed, My only begotten Son is being sown as a seed that will go into the ground and die so that out of that seed will be brought many sons to glory.

My Lamb lies across the sky and covers universes. He has been raised high above all principalities and powers. All power and might and dominion has been given to Him.

I had to find the perfect seed, the Father said, so that many would be brought to perfection. The Lamb, the most Precious of all My animals, the gentlest, had to be the picture of the heart of My Son. Nobody would want to harm a Lamb, they have tender, gentle natures and are full of innocence and joy. But, the Lamb was just the seed.

He was sown in weakness, raised in strength because even as the Lamb was wounded unto death, out of the river of His side came the Lion of the Tribe of Judah. One, Who would rule and reign for eternity. One to Whom every knee would bow and every tongue confess that He is Lord. The gentleness of His nature gave Him high places of authority! He rules and reigns with a sword of pure justice and truth. The scales that He holds in His hands are true, every weight is true and the measurements are of the finest gold tried in the fire. He judges with gentleness and might, with power and truth and the Light of His resurrection glory can cut through and separate the precious from the vile.

Out of the Lamb came the Lion, because the Lamb never lost its nature but the might and Kingship of the Lion was added to It. The perfection of innocence became the perfection of might because it was combined with meekness.

AND He was crowned King of Kings and Lord of Lords and unto Him was given all power and might and dominion for He carries still on Himself His wounds unto death, but He was raised up in great glory, overcoming death for ALL mankind, breaking the power and bondage of it.

If you can just receive it!

"Verily, verily, I say unto you, Except a corn of wheat fall into the ground and die, it abideth alone: but if it die, it bringeth forth much fruit" (John 12:24).

"And Abraham lifted up his eyes, and looked, and behold behind him a ram caught in a thicket by his horns: and Abraham went

and took the ram, and offered him up for a burnt offering in the stead of his son" (Genesis 22:13).

"He was oppressed, and he was afflicted, yet he opened not his mouth: he is brought as a lamb to the slaughter, and as a sheep before her shearers is dumb, so he openeth not his mouth" (Isaiah 53:7).

"It is sown in dishonour; it is raised in glory: it is sown in weakness; it is raised in power" (1 Corinthians 15:43).

"And one of the elders saith unto me, Weep not: behold, the Lion of the tribe of Juda, the Root of David, hath prevailed to open the book, and to loose the seven seals thereof...Saying with a loud voice, Worthy is the Lamb that was slain to receive power, and riches, and wisdom, and strength, and honour, and glory, and blessing" (Revelation 5:5,12).

"That at the name of Jesus every knee should bow, of things in heaven, and things in earth, and things under the earth" (Philippians 2:10).

"And he hath on his vesture and on his thigh a name written, KING OF KINGS, AND LORD OF LORDS" (Revelation 19:16).

29

GETHSEMANE

What can I tell you about Gethsemane? It is the place where the flesh is dealt with in a final blow. It is the meeting place where My will, the will of the Almighty, becomes the oil press that crushes until flesh gives way to the fullness of My will and purposes. Gethsemane, the mighty oil press comes down to the one that has already begun to break, that has faced storm after storm for Me and then reaches out in a final struggle to receive strength to do all My will. The 'weight of purpose,' together with the struggle brings about the fulfillment of purpose.

The struggle was so severe for My Son that the capillaries in His forehead began to break down through the intensity of the pressure of His emotions and His mental agony. The blood began to seep into His sweat glands and He began to perspire and the perspiration appeared as drops of blood. His foreknowledge of the suffering that He would have to go through reached the point of climax where He had to choose His will or Mine. As God, His will was already knit with Mine. As Man, He had to suffer the worst mental agony that any human being could ever suffer, so that He could overcome it and mankind could be released from every mental agony ever suffered.

The matter of the will: The will is such a powerful force that it has devoured nations and peoples. It had to be conquered and it was! At Gethsemane, Jesus set His face as flint to do My will, even as in His humanity He cried out to be released from that cup of suffering, His face was set as flint. The struggle between spirit and flesh ensued and as I saw that it was so intense that He became weak I sent an angel to strengthen Him. He used this strength to empower His Spirit and not His flesh. He could have taken this angelic strength as so many have and used it to strengthen Himself and stand up against Me and say, "No!" come up with another plan. But, He took that strength and prayed even harder for My will to be done and in doing so He opened a portal of grace and power that had been closed to mankind since the fall.

Gethsemane is the reason that you can turn away from your own desires and set your face as flint to follow Me. Gethsemane is the reason that your breakthrough is only a veil, a membrane away and not a shut door that you have to break down. My Son did it and He had His eyes on your face as He fought this battle. In His omnipotence and omnipresence the faces of the Sons of Glory appeared before Him and as He saw you, His heart melted, His will broke and He surrendered to His purpose. The last frontier, the final conquest, the most outlying territory can only be captured because of love.

The breaking of a will has a sound to it. In the spirit realm it has the sound of a sledge hammer coming down on a rock. As the will is broken bringing it into surrender, the spirit of that person is released from an area of captivity – it is a sound of victory, a sound of triumph because now one has entered into the rhythms and timings of Heaven and has discovered their true purpose.

"And he was withdrawn from them about a stone's cast, and kneeled down, and prayed, Saying, Father, if thou be willing, remove this cup from me: nevertheless not my will, but thine, be done. And there appeared an angel unto him from heaven, strengthening him. And being in an agony he prayed more earnestly: and his sweat was as it were great drops of blood falling down to the ground" (Luke 22:41-44).

30

HE EVER LIVETH TO MAKE INTERCESSION FOR US

hen My Son stood up and said, "Here am I send Me!" He was reflecting the heart of a great intercessor. His heart was so moved by compassion in that moment in eternity that He was willing to give it all to save that which was lost and because of His response He set in motion the timings of His destiny. You see, He had already been slain, in His nature as the Lamb. He had already looked forward and seen His Blood shed for many, but He had to reach the defining moment of saying, "Here am I send Me!"

Even though He was God and had created the world and mankind with Me, He still had the freedom to choose. Even though He was the Lamb slain from the foundation of the world, at any moment He could choose to stop the process of redemption, which started with intercession, and just enjoy His throne. The world would still have gone on, universe would still have traveled their pathways but Hell would have enlarged its borders as millions upon millions of people would have coursed through its gates.

Compassion moved His heart, it is the nature of the Godhead. It is what makes Us God like no other god, it is the difference between Us and the gods of the heathen. We, ourselves, stepped in to save those who had offended Us. We reached out to the ones that offended Our purity and holiness and made a way for transformation. The price was unspeakably great. My Son had to suffer intensely at the hand of His creation, and We, the Holy Spirit and I missed His sweet Presence during His sojourn on earth. Not only that, but because We are One, as He suffered, We suffered too.

When He cried, "It is finished," when He held the keys to Death, Hell and the Grave, when He resurrected from the dead and had His glorified body and sat down at My right hand of power, He could have said, "Now I can rest and enjoy My throne" but, He never rescinded on His High Priestly duties. He ever liveth to make intercession!

The heart of an intercessor is not for high position, but to rule and reign in order to ordain the events of man that he may rescue him from his situation and even from himself. His every word, his every tear, his every movement is ordained for the purpose of redemption and the cost is death to himself that he might bring life to others.

Your High Priest lives in the highest of realms not because He is God, but because He has no thought for Himself. When He prays He intercedes with the mind of the Godhead and decrees the purposes of the Godhead on the earth and in the lives of man. It is His nature that makes Him an intercessor because He is the Mercy Seat! When you become the Mercy Seat on earth, your intercessions will become limitless, but until you do your vision and perceptions will be tainted and your emotions will follow your vision and your intercession will be limited.

You are hidden in your High Priest, Christ, as He sits on His throne, He carries you ever before My throne of grace, as you are in Him, let Him teach you to intercede as He does. He knows the rhythms of the earth and the Heavens. He wrote the Books of Destiny with Me and when He prays, every angel involved in that distinct purpose is alerted. Every material thing involved comes together to bring about the purpose in His prayer, that is why you never have to worry about finances when you are in My will. You have an intercessor in Heaven Who was tempted in every way possible while He was on earth, so you know that He understands what you go through and will pray for you to overcome as He did.

When you seek to know His heart and you join with Him in a divine union of prayer Heaven and earth will be moved and mountains will move at your word because your mouth and His are one. You will be caught up and taken out of your dimension because as you change dimensions your perspective changes and you look through eternal paradigms, which are limitless. The pattern, which has been set on earth for judging certain situations changes, and so your thought patterns begin to conform to Mine and you pray My will.

Do not seek to have compassion through human understanding, but ask My Son for His heart in every situation. Become the Mercy Seat on the earth and you will find the Shekinah of My Presence begins to dwell with you, My intercessor, My representative on the earth.

"But this man, because he continueth ever, hath an unchangeable priesthood. Wherefore he is able also to save them to the uttermost that come unto God by him, seeing he ever liveth to make intercession for them" (Hebrews 7:24-25).

"For in that he himself hath suffered being tempted, he is able to succour them that are tempted" (Hebrews 2:18).

Part Two

THE TRANSFORMING POWER OF THE BLOOD OF CHRIST

A BIBLE STUDY

TABLE OF CONTENTS

TABLE OF CONTENTS
(Continued)

CHAPTER

THE BEGINNING –
WHERE IT ALL STARTED!

When we begin to teach or talk about the Blood of Jesus Christ we are touching something very precious to God, that is highly regarded in Heaven and if it is highly regarded in Heaven, it must be highly regarded in the earth by God's people. We do not want to take it lightly but let us give honour to the precious Blood of the Son of God. We are bought with a very high price, our whole lives are bought with it, every person on the earth can be bought with it. I believe that the angels gathered up every drop of Blood after Jesus died so that not one drop of His pure Blood would be trampled upon. The Blood of God's sinless Son was the most precious of all Blood because it was and is pure light.

To have a good overall understanding about the Blood of Christ, we have to lay a foundation that will bring clarity, we must understand what happened in the Garden of Eden, what happened to Adam and his wife Eve, and the way in which it affected all of us.

GOD CREATED MAN AFTER HIS OWN IMAGE

"And God said, Let us make man in our image, after our likeness: and let them have dominion over the fish of the sea, and over the fowl of the air, and over the cattle, and over all the earth, and over every creeping thing that creepeth upon the earth. So God created man in his own image, in the image of God created he him; male and female created he them" (Genesis 1:26, 27).

" And the Lord God formed man of the dust of the ground, and breathed into his nostrils the breath of life; and man became a living soul" (Genesis 2:7).

God created man in His own image and then gave him His own life by breathing into him. The old Jewish writers believe that God breathed into Adam three times for body, soul and spirit. Man was created with God's own hands and breath.

Everything else was created because God said, *"Let there be…"*

When God breathes that breath never ends, it is eternal, it holds no death in it. When God breathed into Adam there was no death in that breath. When He said, *"Let there be Light"* the Light that was in Him came out of Him in the form of words and began to create and has never stopped creating. Stars are still being born, galaxies still being created, and so much else that we know nothing about. New discoveries are being made everyday. It will be so exciting to look into the books of the mysteries of creation when we get to Heaven, perhaps God will even allow us a sneak preview while we are still on the earth. I would love that, wouldn't you?

The word for *breathed* in the Hebrew (5301) is "Nephach," which also means "to kindle."

By this we understand that the fire of God's own love, His glory, **kindled or ignited life** within Adam and that is what Adam carried within him when he became a living being, a *"nephesh."*

"He that loveth not knoweth not God; for God is love" (1 John 4:8).

This verse tells us that God IS love – it is not a part of His character – it is Who He is.

Jesus, Who is the *"express image"* of His Father said in John 8:12, *"I am the Light of the world..."* In John 14:6, He says of Himself, *"...I am the way, the truth, and the life:..."*

God breathed into Adam, Love, Life and Light – everything that He is! The Glory was within him sustaining his life and his relationship with God. He was "stuff" of God's "stuff," he had within him God's DNA, he became a part of God's generations. God does nothing by chance, this was all part of a plan formed from within the council of the Godhead. When God looked at Adam He not only saw him but He saw us, just as when He looked at Abraham He saw countless generations of his descendants.

> *...the fire and the Glory of God, like liquid love, traveled throughout his body, it traveled throughout his veins.*

When God kindled or ignited Adam, the fire and Glory of God, like liquid love, travelled throughout his body, it travelled throughout his veins and we have to believe that Adam had a body somewhat like ours and this fire went into every cell of his own being. As it traveled it ignited the creativity of God and the inspiration and ability of God within him so that he could do whatever and know whatever he needed to do and to know. That living God-part of

Adam was alive within him so that Adam could co-operate with the Creator. God breathed all that He is into Adam.

"And they were both naked, the man and his wife, and were not ashamed" (Genesis 2:25).

"The spirit of man is the candle of the Lord, searching all the inward parts of the belly" (Proverbs 20:27).

The candle of the Lord, their spirits, shone brightly with God's Glory and that Glory searched out every part of Adam and Eve, and all that was found within their inward parts was innocence. There was no guile or lust in them – they looked with pure eyes of innocence. They were not ashamed because shame did not exist in their world.

> *Adam carried the fullnesss of the Glory that he was created for and so there was no resistance in his fellowship with God.*

Adam carried the Glory of God within him and it shone out of him, through his body that God had formed out of the dust, and the Glory covered him, so that he could relate to God. There was a likeness between them that brought about a relationship, Adam's life came out of God. Both Adam and his wife, Eve, were naked but there was a radiance, which radiated out from within them. That radiance of the Glory of God was not only a protective covering over them but became the meeting place where Adam and God could connect, relate and walk together. It was an exchange of light for light, Glory for Glory. Adam carried the fullness of the Glory that he was created for and so there was no resistance in his fellowship with God.

God gave Adam and Eve dominion over all that He had created in the earth, He gave him the power to rule. He made him the keeper of the garden (Genesis 1:27-30) and then He brought every living creature to Adam to see what he would name them (Genesis 2:19-20). Can you imagine what it must have been like for God to see His creation, Adam, functioning in His own creativity? He knew every creature, named every creature, and had authority over them, and, having authority, would care for their well-being. He was like his Creator who takes care of the fowls of the air and the lilies of the field. The best part of Adam's day must have been when he went walking with God. AND God put the whole universe on automatic pilot – just so that He could go for a walk with Adam!

SIN INTRODUCED TO MANKIND BY THE FIRST ADAM

"And when the woman saw that the tree was good for food, and that it was pleasant to the eyes, and a tree to be desired to make one wise, she took of the fruit thereof, and did eat, and gave also unto her husband with her; and he did eat. And the eyes of them both were opened, and they knew that they were naked; and they sewed fig leaves together, and made themselves aprons" (Genesis 3:6-7).

There was a tree in the Garden of Eden called the Tree of the Knowledge of Good and Evil. God had given Adam specific instructions concerning not eating from this tree – *"...thou shalt not eat of it: for in the day that thou eatest thereof thou shalt surely die"* (Genesis 2:16-17). The enemy spoke beguilingly to Eve saying that if they ate of that tree their eyes would be opened and they would be as gods knowing good and evil (Genesis 3:5). The word for "gods" in this scripture means those who judge by weighing knowledge in the balance. This was the point at which man began to walk by

101

weighing knowledge in the balance, looking at *his* options, rather than seeking to know God's will in every situation.

When they ate, the Glory of the Lord departed from them. Their eyes were now seeing through the guile in their hearts and they could see their nakedness. The Glory of God could not remain where there was disobedience and sin.

We know that when man sinned he lost the covering of the Glory and fellowship with God was broken. But, what happened to that which was within his body that sustained life? What happened to that which God breathed into him that provided love, light and life to every part of the living being that God had formed out of the dust?

That which was a flowing river of light began to slow down and bunch together and became the kind of blood that we know today,

Scientists many years ago began an extensive study of the blood and its peculiar quality of maintaining life, they began to discover that blood is actually made up of congealed or coagulated light. I am referring here to our blood. They have also found that right at the center of a blood corpuscle is a little spark of light. They tell us that every cell of our body as it metabolises gives off a spark of light and I believe that is what is left from the days of the glory that man once carried.

When Adam sinned what happened to the glory of God that was within him? I believe that which was a flowing river of Light began to slow down and bunch together and became the kind of blood that we know today. Instead of being pure light and glory it became red and it formed blood clots. It is like light that has been put under a bushel. Maybe that is why Jesus says, don't put your light under a bushel but be like a beacon on a hill because when we go back to carrying the Light of the world, we go back to that place that we had with God and then people are drawn to Him through our light. And so, man's blood took on a whole different aspect.

THE FIRST SACRIFICE – GOD PROVIDES A COVERING

Genesis 3:9-11: *And the Lord God called unto Adam, and said unto him, Where art thou? And he said, I heard thy voice in the garden, and I was afraid, because I was naked; and I hid myself. And he said, Who told thee that thou wast naked? Hast thou eaten of the tree, whereof I commanded thee that thou shouldest not eat?*

Immediately after Adam sinned God felt the break in fellowship because there was no longer the connection through the glory. Perhaps it was at the moment that he ate of the fruit, or perhaps it was the moment that it became the intent of his heart. Why did Jesus teach that if you have thought about the act of sin it is as though you have already done it?

When God called for Adam, He knew that Adam was not coming, He was not caught unaware but He felt the pain of the loss of fellowship through Adam's rebellion. Yet, He kept His rendezvous in the cool of the evening. His heart was broken as He called out for Adam. It was from a heart of longing that already missed the fellowship of the man He had created for that very purpose. When He asked, "Where are you?" it was a question that went beyond asking about Adam's location. Adam had now entered into another Kingdom, the kingdom of darkness and needed to be saved out of it.

This is the same God that wrote the Song of Songs through Solomon, declaring His love for the Shulamite – *"You have ravished my heart..."* (Song of Songs 4:9).

At the heart of the matter was did they trust God? Who did they choose to believe when the accusation came against God? Was God afraid that they would become gods just as He was God? Is that why He did not want them eating from the Tree of the Knowledge of Good and Evil?

Although God loved Adam still, there was now no intimacy and God in His righteousness had to make declarations of sorrows to come for the Race of Adam, the earth and the Enemy.

"Unto Adam also and to his wife did the Lord God make coats of skins, and clothed them" (Genesis 3:12).

The word "make" (6213) is the Hebrew word *"asah"* which means to "make, toil, labor" but it also means to "offer" or "sacrifice."

The word for "skins" (5785) is the Hebrew word *"or"* which can mean the skin of man or the hide of an animal usually after it is skinned.

Reading this scripture we understand that God Himself sacrificed an animal in order to make coats to cover both Adam and Eve to hide their nakedness. That means that blood had to have been shed. Although God made them coats of skins it was the blood that covered their sins.

In all of this we see the following:

1. This was the first example of a sacrifice in which blood was shed because of sin.

2. The innocent died for the guilty.

3   Something beloved had to die. The animal had to have been loved by Adam because he had dominion over the animals and was responsible for its care. That which was precious had to be sacrificed!

4.   The shed blood provided a covering that would hide Adam and Eve's nakedness and give them protection as they left the garden.

5.   Adam and Eve learnt the price of sin and that it could only be atoned for by the shedding of innocent blood.

6.   They would teach the same thing to their descendants.

This was the Adamic Covenant

CHAPTER

2

IN HIS JUDGMENT, GOD REMEMBERS MERCY

"O Lord, I have heard thy speech, and was afraid: O Lord, revive thy work in the midst of the years, in the midst of the years make known; in wrath remember mercy" (Habakkuk 3:2).

"For he shall have judgment without mercy, that hath shewed no mercy; and mercy rejoiceth against judgment" (James 2:13).

Mercy rejoices against judgment! What beautiful words. Even though Adam and Eve had opened up a realm of darkness to themselves, God, in His great love provided a way for them to be protected and provided a way that they could maintain contact with Him. These two scriptures contain the cry of the Spirit revealing God's own heart. Mercy was shown, but Adam and Eve could never enter into the Garden of Eden again. There was relationship without the intimacy that comes through the glory.

"For the law having a shadow of good things to come, and not the very image of the things, can never with those sacrifices which they offered year by year continually make the comers thereunto perfect. For then would they not have ceased to be offered? because that the worshippers once purged should have had no more conscience of sins" (Hebrews 10:1-2).

God initiated the first sacrifice; it was the stronger showing mercy to the weaker who had transgressed against Him. But, the blood sacrifices for sin lacked one thing – **they could not purge the conscience.** The sacrifices had to be made again and again, but the memory of the sin remained in the conscience.

CAIN AND ABEL

"And Adam knew Eve his wife; and she conceived, and bare Cain, and said, I have gotten a man from the Lord. And she again bare his brother Abel. And Abel was a keeper of sheep, but Cain was a tiller of the ground. And in process of time it came to pass, that Cain brought of the fruit of the ground an offering unto the Lord. And Abel, he also brought of the firstlings of his flock and of the fat thereof. And the **Lord had respect unto Abel and to his offering:** *But unto Cain and to his offering he had not respect. And Cain was very wroth, and his countenance fell"* (Genesis 4:1-5).

The words "had respect" in the Hebrew mean "to turn around and gaze in amazement."

God saw the blood as Abel offered the first fruits of his flock and it drew in His attention. He turned around and gazed in amazement at the very first blood offered to Him. Abel had learned the divine law of a life for a life, **only** the life in the blood could redeem his sin.

This was more than just an offering, it revealed a heart that was willing to do things God's way. Abel had a different spirit. He farmed sheep even though in those days they did not eat meat, eating meat only came after the flood. Why would he do that? Perhaps he wanted to be always ready with his offering.

Abel had learned that only the life in the blood could redeem his sin. His offering revealed a heart that was willing to do things God's way.

"For the life of the flesh is in the blood: and I have given it to you upon the altar to make an atonement for your souls: for it is the blood that maketh an atonement for the soul" (Leviticus 17:11).

God ignored Cain's offering – the fruit of the ground was not acceptable as a covering for sin, just as the fig leaves were not acceptable in the garden when Cain's parents tried to cover themselves with them. Cain was careless with God, he wanted to do it his own way!

I can just hear their mother, Eve, telling them, "The fig leaves didn't do it, vegetation is not an acceptable covering – it had to be blood! In those days, even though we were brilliant, we did not understand how multi-faceted God is. We should have just trusted Him, if we had we would still have been there in that beautiful place, but now we know, **God requires blood.**"

These two brothers are a picture to us of the conflict between our own soul and spirit. The spirit wants to obey God and come into a place of communion with Him. The spirit, which is eternal, longs to once again be filled with the glory of God and to dwell always in

His courts, but our soul loves to have its own way, to do things its own way and to be its own little god. So, within ourselves we see the same conflict and characteristics that we see in those brothers. The question is; which one will win? Will the soul finally acknowledge its defeat? When it does, we will walk in the realms of glory that Adam did and perhaps beyond.

> *"And the Lord said unto Cain, Why art thou wroth? and why is thy countenance fallen? If thou doest well, shalt thou not be accepted? and if thou doest not well, sin lieth at the door. And unto thee shall be his desire, and thou shalt rule over him. And Cain talked with Abel his brother: and it came to pass, when they were in the field, that Cain rose up against Abel his brother, and slew him. And the Lord said unto Cain, Where is Abel thy brother? And he said, I know not: Am I my brother's keeper? And he said, What hast thou done? The voice of thy brother's blood crieth unto me from the ground"* (Genesis 4:6-10).

The life in Abel's blood cried out for vengeance. There was a voice in that blood. Abel gave God what He wanted. It was not only his sacrifice that was excellent but he did the right thing because he believed God! He trusted God.

> *"By faith Abel offered unto God a more excellent sacrifice than Cain, by which he obtained witness that he was righteous, God testifying of his gifts: and by it he being dead yet speaketh"* (Hebrews 11:4).

God heard Abel's blood crying out from the ground because there was life in it. Do not eat blood because you are eating the life of another. Abel had cleansed himself with the blood sacrifice so in God's eyes he was innocent and that innocent blood cried out. The blood of Abel was telling God what had happened. It not only had a sound but the light in the blood shone up from the earth. Even in these days, where there has been a crime, infrared red lights are used by investigating agents to expose blood stains.

Genesis 4:11 tells us that the earth opened its mouth to receive Abel's blood. God created the earth and it had compassion on Abel and received his blood. We do not understand the cohesion between nature and ourselves. Nature should respond to our words. We can decree and be spared many things as those that are righteous through the Blood of Christ. Earth – be at peace! We need to proclaim it especially where we live. We have to walk the land noting where our feet are stepping and claim it for Jesus Christ. If the earth can open up to receive Abel's blood surely it can close up so that our blood is not shed. The earth is groaning with the weight of sin but if we can stand in the place of Christ on the earth, in a place of intercession for the people, will God not hear the voice that cries out from this earth and stand and gaze in amazement at us? "My daughter is standing there when the earthquake is coming and she is claiming my peace on the land. I am going to honor her faith."

Anything short of absolute glory and absolute perfection needs a blood covering and a sacrifice.

Some years ago we were alerted to a tornado in our area of Jasper, Arkansas. We made preparation for a place of safety in the natural, but a few of us went outside and began to rebuke the tornado and took authority over our area refusing to allow it on our property and allow it to cause any damage. One young man had a shofar and blew it. We heard that well-described sound of a freight train coming, that was pretty scary, and went back inside. Nothing happened! Everything was quiet. Later we found out that the tornado as it was heading towards us made a 90 degree turn. Its pathway could be clearly seen by the devastation it left as it went through the trees. God heard our cry and so did that tornado!

Abel did not realize that he was part of a pattern that God was developing – part of a picture bigger than himself and that in this century his voice would still be speaking.

Right in the beginning God laid out a foundation for man when he began to provide man with a covering other than the glory. The Bible tells us that all have sinned and fallen short of the glory. Anything short of absolute glory and absolute perfection needs a blood covering and a sacrifice.

A Fountain of Cleansing

There is a fountain filled with blood, (Verse 1)
Drawn from Emmanuel's veins
And sinners plunged beneath that flood
Lose all their guilty stains

Dear dying Lamb! Thy precious blood (Verse 4)
Shall never lose its power,
Till all the ransomed church of God
Be saved to sin no more.

E'er since by faith I saw the stream (Verse 5)
Thy flowing wounds supply
Redeeming love has been my theme
And shall be till I die.

William Cowper (1772)

Whenever the Blood is taught the great cloud of witnesses come to listen and the mighty hosts of angels want to hear the Word and hear about the Blood. They know that Jesus' Blood was not shed for them; but they want to hear how

Jesus, their Master, redeemed mankind through His Blood. The Lord of Hosts Who is their Leader.

From time immemorial there has been a fascination with blood. People are either drawn to it or repulsed by it. There are even those that faint at the sight of it. These days there is fear attached to it because of the virulent AIDS virus. It has been studied, analysed, used to save lives and by the shedding of it a life can be taken. We hear of bloodshed in the news every day; murder, war, fighting, killing, shooting. It has been the subject of movies, where thrill-seekers can go, and somehow the sight of it is dangerously exciting. What is it that causes us to react at the sight of blood? Somehow, instinctively, we know that when a body loses blood it loses life.

God created this life-giving, mysterious substance. It either connects us to Him or separates us from Him. To God, according to the Bible, blood speaks of: Justification; atonement; reconciliation; cleansing; transformation; power to overcome; authority; destruction of the works of the enemy; covenant.

COMPOSITION OF THE BLOOD

Most of us have five quarts, consisting of red and white blood corpuscles or cells that are carried around our body in plasma which is a liquid consisting mostly of water. Our blood reaches every part of our body and interacts with every cell. It goes into all of our organs, bones, heart, lungs and into the cells of our flesh. It feeds, cleanses and protects us – white blood cells and antibodies will fight whatever tries to invade our body to bring harm. The red blood cells carry oxygen to each cell and remove carbon dioxide.

If we are sick we put medication into the blood and it will take that medication into every part of our body, into every cell to bring healing.

The Blood of Jesus does the same!! The Blood of Jesus cleanses and renews not only our soul, it will bring healing and the breath of God to every cell in our entire body.

"And all that dwell upon the earth shall worship him, whose names are not written in the book of life of the Lamb slain from the foundation of the world" (Revelation 13:8).

God had a plan before Adam because He foresaw the future, but out of His great love He created man even though within man was the ability to make the wrong choice.

"And God said, Let us make man in our image, after our likeness: and let them have dominion over the fish of the sea, and over the fowl of the air, and over the cattle, and over all the earth, and over every creeping thing that creepeth upon the earth" (Genesis 1:26).

The Blood of Jesus will bring healing and the breath of God to every cell in your entire body.

When God said, *"Let Us make man in Our Image,"* it was the beginning of the release of the well-laid plan of the ages. The Hebrew word, Elohim, denotes "gods" in the plural. The "Us" that God was referring to is the Godhead; which we know to be made up of God, the Father; Jesus Christ, the Son; and the Holy Spirit, Who all interact together and function as One. The use of "Us" here also puts us in memory of the royal courts in the nations that still have a monarchy, where "us" and "we" are used as a sign of majesty and respect.

But, within the "Us" in this verse, was *"The Lamb that was slain from the foundation of the world."*

Jesus, in one of His discussions with the Jews said to them, *"…Verily, verily, I say unto you, Before Abraham was, I am"* (John 8:58).

He was pointing out to them that He has always existed. This is hard for us to understand as we live in a past, present and future world. We need a revelation of the timelessness of God because at the time of creation Jesus had already been slain as the sacrificial lamb **when there was nobody to slay Him.**

BY WHOM WAS HE SLAIN?

"All we like sheep have gone astray; we have turned every one to his own way; and the Lord hath laid on him the iniquity of us all" (Isaiah 53:6).

"Yet it pleased the Lord to bruise him; he hath put him to grief: when thou shalt make his soul an offering for sin, he shall see his seed, he shall prolong his days, and the pleasure of the Lord shall prosper in his hand" (Isaiah 53:10).

"For Christ also hath once suffered for sins, the just for the unjust, that he might bring us to God, being put to death in the flesh, but quickened by the Spirit" (1 Peter 3:18).

"…the Lord hath laid on him…" — *"…it pleased the Lord to bruise him…"* — *"…the just for the unjust…"*

These scriptures give us a picture of the total co-operation between the Godhead, the "one mind" of the plan of redemption.

The just **Son** having the iniquity of the world placed on Him unjustly, to accept the punishment God's justice demands.

The **Father** revealing His heart for unjust sinners in laying the iniquities on His own Son.

The **Spirit** quickening the dead body of the Son.

Jesus was the seed laid in the "ground" (so to speak) to die so that many might live. The Father willingly laid on His Son the sins and iniquities of the whole world, past, present and future in a way that only the Eternal God could and His Son willingly carried them because it was the most unique plan of the ages. Man was unable to help himself, he had bowed to his own will and desires and had become ensnared in a dark kingdom. He lived in the realm of his soul without enlightenment.

THE GREAT DIVINE PURPOSE

The release of that which the sinless, guileless, innocent Lamb of God carried within His veins – **His Blood,** which would cover the sins of mankind so that they were never to be remembered again. Where there was loss of the glory and character of God by man, there would be restoration of the glory and restoration of intimacy with the Father. The plan was not just so that man could be cleansed from sin, but the covering of the glory would translate him into heavenly places where man could be seated with Christ.

"All we like sheep have gone astray; we have turned every one to his own way; and the LORD hath laid on him the iniquity of us all" (Isaiah 53:6).

It was "done," it was "finished" from the *"foundation of the world"* – **when the plans were laid.**

116

THE MYSTERY

"For the life of the flesh is in the blood: and I have given it to you upon the altar to make an atonement for your souls: for it is the blood that maketh an atonement for the soul" (Leviticus 17:11).

God tells us very clearly why sacrifices are made: *"For the life of the flesh is in the blood."*

It takes LIFE to counteract the death caused by sin. It takes eternal life to counteract death eternally. When sinless blood is shed, eternity is opened up because there is no death in it.

"And almost all things are by the law purged with blood; and without shedding of blood is no remission" (Hebrews 9:22).

This scripture tells us that everything has to be cleansed by blood or it retains its quality of sin. When there is death in our blood in the natural, fresh or healthy blood provides life. Jesus' Blood is always fresh and life-giving; it cleanses every area of our lives. It took the purest and greatest kind of love for the Creator to willingly sacrifice Himself by giving Himself into the hands of His creation and allowing them to put Him through trials and kill Him in the most tortuous way. John heard Jesus say it and it rang in His heart, so He recorded it for all of us, down through the generations, to read. The heart of God Himself was expressed in the verse below.

> *It takes eternal life to counteract death eternally.*
>
> *When sinless blood is shed, eternity is opened up because there is no death in it.*

117

Jesus said: "Greater love hath no man than this, that a man lay down his life for his friends" (John 15:13).

Not only was that great love, but He also laid down His life knowing that we would become His friends through His sacrifice. Friends are closer than servants, they care what one thinks and about one's feelings. When everyone else leaves, they are still there because they know your heart.

A FOUNTAIN OPENS UP

"In that day there shall be a fountain opened to the house of David and to the inhabitants of Jerusalem for sin and for uncleanness" (Zechariah 13:1).

"And I will pour upon the house of David, and upon the inhabitants of Jerusalem, the spirit of grace and of supplications: and they shall look upon me whom they have pierced, and they shall mourn for him, as one mourneth for his only son, and shall be in bitterness for him, as one that is in bitterness for his firstborn" (Zechariah 12:10).

God opened up the curtains of time and showed Zechariah the future. The House of David and the inhabitants of Jerusalem would look, the Amplified Bible says, "earnestly," upon Him and the realization of what happened in the days of their forefathers would send them into extraordinary mourning. They would realise that the Messiah they were waiting for had already come and what was done to Him. But, in the midst of it all, there would be a fountain of cleansing made available for them.

THE INVITATION

"Come now, and let us reason together, saith the Lord: though your sins be as scarlet, they shall be as white as snow; though they be red like crimson, they shall be as wool" (Isaiah 1:18).

"And when I passed by thee, and saw thee polluted in thine own blood, I said unto thee when thou wast in thy blood, Live; yea, I said unto thee when thou wast in thy blood, Live" (Ezekiel 16:6).

When the Holy Spirit sees one soaked in the Word and soaked in the Blood, He cannot resist it --

HE COMES!

God is talking to Jerusalem, saying that she is one that came out of ungodly roots and that when He found her she was lying in her natal blood, the blood of her birth. But God picked her up and said, "LIVE!"

God picked us up out of the blood of our roots, the blood of our birth with every generational sin in it and said, "I am going to put you into the fountain that I have opened up and wash away every part of that which is causing your blood to stick because it is congealed and heavy with sin and cover you with the Blood of My Own Spotless Lamb so that you can know Me."

"Now when I passed by thee, and looked upon thee, behold, thy time was the time of love; and I spread my skirt over thee, and covered thy nakedness: yea, I sware unto thee, and entered into a covenant with thee, saith the Lord God, and thou becamest mine. Then washed I thee with water; yea, I throughly washed away thy blood from thee, and I anointed thee with oil" (Ezekiel 16:8-9).

119

God is saying that when you grew up and were ready for love, I came to you and covered you. I put my mantle over you. I loved you so passionately that I vowed to you that I would love you forever, I entered into a marriage covenant with you and I became yours and you became Mine. I washed your guilt away with water, I cleaned you up and then I anointed you with anointing oil.

"For there are three that bear record in heaven, the Father, the Word, and the Holy Ghost: and these three are one. And there are three that bear witness in earth, the spirit, and the water, and the blood: and these three agree in one" (1 John 5:7-8).

> *That fountain takes us into God dimensions that vibrate with Light and Sound because the Blood of Jesus is full of Light and Sound.*

There is such an agreement in Heaven which is made manifest on the earth between the Water and the Blood and the Spirit that when the Holy Spirit sees one soaked in the Word and soaked in the Blood, He cannot resist it – HE COMES!

When a woman gives birth the child goes through the birth canal and blood comes forth. The Blood of Christ pushes us through the birth canal in Heavenly places and we are birthed out of the natural realm into a realm of the Spirit where we are born into the family of God. We thus become royalty and can walk without shame. Everything of the past is left in the grave of who we were. We are now able to walk in newness of life, rejoicing in the Lamb slain from the foundation of the world.

These are GOD things, these are the workings of the universe they are not just a good plan. It is the way the universe works because

God set every thing in order and He sets the rhythms of the universe and we are part of that universe. The minute we get into that fountain, we belong to the same dimensions as God.

God has translated us out of the kingdom of darkness into the Kingdom of His dear Son. That fountain takes us into God dimensions that vibrate with Light and Sound because the Blood of Jesus is full of Light and Sound. We, as members of His Kingdom, no longer give off the sound of darkness and the sound of discord because we do not agree with God, because we are weighing our own options rather than submitting to God's perfect will for our lives.

If we can only GET IT!! That God loves us passionately enough to open up a fountain of cleansing out of the veins of His Own Son.

The Blood only has authority where it has cleansed.

WHO IS JESUS THAT HIS BLOOD SHOULD BE SO POWERFUL?

*I*n Leviticus 17:11 God told us that LIFE is in the blood, so the quality of the life affects the blood. That Blood or that life has to be laid out on an altar for atonement to happen. It is Who Jesus Is that makes His Blood powerful!!

> *"And I heard a loud voice saying in heaven, Now is come salvation, and strength, and the kingdom of our God, and the power of his Christ: for the accuser of our brethren is cast down, which accused them before our God day and night. And they overcame him by the blood of the Lamb, and by the word of their testimony; and they loved not their lives unto the death"* (Revelation 12:10-11).

The voice in Heaven, of one of our brethren, is giving a proclamation that says that the Accuser of the Brethren is cast down!

The first thing they overcame him with is the Blood of the Lamb and because of the Blood of the Lamb they had a word of testimony and could love not their lives unto death!

We do not have to worry about the Accuser of the brethren; the Blood of the Lamb has already overcome him we just have to believe it!

When I was a very new Christian I had just moved into my own home and was looking for some furniture. The friend that I was visiting had a neighbour that was selling an armchair. She said that it was probably exactly what I was looking for but warned me that the man attended spiritualist meetings. I was so caught up in all that Jesus had done for me that I was not concerned about it. I went to see the man and asked him about his chair and then started to tell him that I had just given my life to the Lord and everything that He had done for me. My testimony set the man on a rampage about all the harm that Christians had done and went on into a history of the crusades. I really did not know what to do and how to answer him and then the Holy Spirit gave me the answer, I asked him what he thought about the Blood of Jesus. The minute I mentioned that the man started shaking and stuttering and had to leave the room until he became composed again, then came back and asked me to leave.

Life is in the blood, so the quality of the life affects the blood.

Needless to say, I did not buy that chair, which was a good thing, as I probably would have got more than I had bargained for. But, I did learn about the incredible overcoming power of the Blood of Jesus!

If there is overcoming power in the Blood of Jesus, then there are characteristics that we need to know about Him.

WHO IS JESUS?

"In the beginning was the Word, and the Word was with God, and the Word was God. The same was in the beginning with God. All things were made by him; and without him was not any thing made that was made. In him was life; and the life was the light of men" (John 1:1-4).

The word for "beginning" in the Greek is "arche" which can mean either a passive beginning or an active cause. In Revelation 1:8, Jesus says: *"I am Alpha and Omega, the beginning and the end, which is, which was, and which is to come, the Almighty."* In other words, He is the "active cause" for everything beginning and being. "Arche" also means extremity or outermost point; also rule, authority, dominion and power.

"And the Word was made flesh, and dwelt among us, and we beheld his glory, the glory as of the only begotten of the Father, full of grace and truth" (John 1:14).

"For God so loved the world, that he gave his only begotten Son, that whosoever believeth in him should not perish, but have everlasting life" (John 3:16).

Only begotten: *monogenes* (Gk) is made up of two words: *Mono* – only, and *genes* – to form or make (this is different from the word *"genneo"* which means to beget. *Monogenes* means the only one that has come out of a particular species.

124

Jesus is always called *"huios"* – the Son of God. *"Huios"* denotes sonship through relationship to the parent not simply through birth.

> *He is from a species or genus that has no beginning and no end. There is no past where He has not been and no future which He does not possess. He IS!*

He is a legitimate offspring that has the moral characteristics of the parent and one that is heir to the Kingdom. Jesus, as the Son of God, expresses His relationship with the Father and reveals that He is the expression of God's character as spoken of in Hebrews 1:3. He expressed grace and truth, light and perfection and in so doing revealed Who His Father was.

Jesus is never called *"teknon"* or child of God, as we are in John 1:12.

"But as many as received him, to them gave he power to become the sons of God, even to them that believe on his name: Which were born, not of blood, nor of the will of the flesh, nor of the will of man, but of God" (John 1:12-13).

This scripture speaks of the sons of God or *"tekna Theou"* – begotten children, those that have received the new birth – with the potential to become sons, that is; those that are led by the Spirit, do God's perfect will and show forth His character. Those that received Him had the "power" to become sons of God. They passed through the spiritual birth canal from one kingdom to the other, to become children of a spiritual being – God the Father. Looking at the son we should see the Father. There should be evidence of the dignity of relationship and likeness to the Father.

When a natural child is born changes take place in the body of the mother causing the child to be pushed through into the world, so Jesus gives us the power to become the children of God with the potential to become sons of God – *"huios."* BUT, we will never be *"monogenes"* – only Jesus is from the species that is God. He is from a species or genus that has no beginning and no end. There is no past where He has not been and no future, which He does not possess. He IS!

"The LORD hath sworn, and will not repent, Thou art a priest for ever after the order of Melchizedek" (Psalm 110:4).

The word, "power" in John 1:12 is the Greek word "exousia" (1849) which means authority, but in the sense that permission has been given and all hindrances removed. The Father Himself authorized us becoming not only His children, but once we were His children, He removed all hindrances to us becoming sons. The Ruler of the universe has given us this permission!

"Wherefore when he cometh into the world, he saith, Sacrifice and offering thou wouldest not, but a body hast thou prepared me" (Hebrews 10:5).

Jesus' Blood came from His Father, it was pure, it was "god" blood. The above verse tells us that God prepared a body for Him. That body was the physical embryo, which went into Mary's womb. He had to be ALL God. In another words He had to have the power to sustain His own life.

Hebrews 7:16 calls it, *"...the power of an endless life."*

Jesus was Mary's *"teknon"*- birthed by her, but He was God's *"Huios"*- His Son and the expression of Himself. Who Jesus is, is very important because His Life is in His Blood.

The following are some points concerning the Blood of Jesus:

1. Within His Blood is the *power of an endless life* – He IS God.

He works within us as a Life. Every time we take communion we are drinking in a Life as we connect with the Blood of Jesus in Heaven.

> *"And they truly were many priests, because they were not suffered to continue by reason of death: But this man, because he continueth ever, hath an unchangeable priesthood"* (Hebrews 7:23, 24).

2. Within His Blood is the Divine Nature

It is the nature of the Lamb who was willing to suffer to redeem back that which was lost. Our hearts are not only washed clean by His Blood but we become partakers of His Divine Nature. The Blood penetrates our whole being reaching down into the inner recesses of our hearts. It is the Blood that gave us our new heart and through it we received these great and precious promises from God.

> *"According as his divine power hath given unto us all things that pertain unto life and godliness, through the knowledge of him that hath called us to glory and virtue: Whereby are given unto us exceeding great and precious promises: that by these ye might be partakers of the divine nature, having escaped the corruption that is in the world through lust"* (2 Peter 1:3).

3. Within His Blood is the Power to overcome.

In the blood of animal sacrifices there is innocence, and innocence was regained, that is why God chose them for atoning sacrifices. But, in the Blood of Jesus there is POWER to overcome.

"And being found in fashion as a man, he humbled himself, and became obedient unto death, even the death of the cross. Wherefore God also hath highly exalted him, and given him a name which is above every name" (Philippians 2:8, 9).

The Blood is our proof that He overcame His own will in the highest way – obedience unto death even the terrible death of the cross, and that He overcame death and rose up with a glorified, resurrected body.

4. The Voice of His Blood cries: *It is finished!*

"But Christ being come an high priest of good things to come, by a greater and more perfect tabernacle, not made with hands, that is to say, not of this building; Neither by the blood of goats and calves, but by his own blood he entered in once into the holy place, having obtained eternal redemption for us" (Hebrews 9:11).

Endless Life

Divine Nature

Power to Overcome

It is Finished!

Mercy

When Jesus gave this cry it resonated throughout Heaven and Hell. The work had been completed! The work by which every man who would come to Him in repentance would have the fullness of righteousness imparted to them through faith. His Blood offering was once and for all! He entered into the Holy Place and sat down, acknowledging that it was all finished. Man no longer had to struggle with sin, but could enter into the rest of faith.

"Let us therefore fear, lest, a promise being left us of entering into his rest, any of you should seem to come short of it. For unto us was the gospel preached, as well as unto them: but the word preached did not profit them, not being mixed with faith in them that heard it. For we which have believed do enter into rest, as he said, As I have sworn in my

> *He has released us from religious rules and ordinances and opened up the way for us to work together with Him.*

wrath, if they shall enter into my rest: although the works were finished from the foundation of the world. For he spake in a certain place of the seventh day on this wise, And God did rest the seventh day from all his works. And in this place again, If they shall enter into my rest. Seeing therefore it remaineth that some must enter therein, and they to whom it was first preached entered not in because of unbelief" (Hebrews 4:1-6).

5. The Voice of His Blood cries for mercy.

"And to Jesus the mediator of the new covenant, and to the blood of sprinkling, that speaketh better things than that of Abel" (Hebrews 12:24).

The New Covenant in His Blood cries out, "Mercy, mercy, mercy!"

The invitation from the Lord Jesus Christ in Matthew 11:28-30 is:

"Come unto me, all ye that labour and are heavy laden, and I will give you rest. Take my yoke upon you, and learn of me; for

I am meek and lowly in heart: and ye shall find rest unto your souls. For my yoke is easy, and my burden is light."

The Message Bible describes "rest" so beautifully as "the unforced rhythms of grace."

His yoke is "easy!" This Greek word, "chrestos" means that it is profitable, kind, gracious and obliging.

When Jesus says that His burden is light, He is saying that no more would mankind be subject to laws and ordinances that would be a weight upon them. No longer would they have to continually be making sacrificial offerings for their sins, but the "burden" would be anything that is on His heart that would be imparted to them, which they could pray through with the help of the Holy Spirit. He has released us from religious rules and ordinances and opened up the way for us to work together with Him. I love to see it this way; the "burden" that He places upon me is the "light" that is going to take Me higher in Him.

THE NOAHIC COVENANT

*I*n the book of Genesis we read that the people of the earth were corrupt before God in the days of Noah and because of that corruption God was going to destroy the earth with a flood. The word for "corrupt" in Genesis 6:11-12 means not only were the inhabitants of the earth corrupt, but they were like "devouring lions," whose corruption had taken over the earth and the earth was full of violence.

A few chapters earlier we read that the sons of God, the fallen angels, had come down and taken the daughters of men as wives because they were fair and the union of the two resulted in giants in the earth. We do not fully understand how this can take place but the Bible tells us that it did. It was a union that "corrupted" the genetic make-up of man resulting in God's decision to destroy them off the face of the earth. These giants were called the Nephillim.

NOAH WAS PERFECT IN HIS GENERATIONS

"These are the generations of Noah: Noah was a just man and perfect in his generations, and Noah walked with God" (Genesis 6:9).

God found in Noah a man that was just and perfect in his generations. It meant that Noah lived a moral life acceptable in every way to the Lord, but also meant that Noah and his past generations had not defiled themselves with those that had come out of the angel and human union. They were still a pure race, created in the image of God, those with whom God could still have fellowship, who could walk with Him.

It was of the utmost importance that there be a race whose lives were redeemable with blood, because the blood of the atoning sacrifices could not be applied to any other race but the race of Man. Redemption was for Man alone!

Redemption was for man alone!

Jesus was to come down through Noah's line and as Saviour of mankind, could not come through a compromised bloodline, that is, a mixing of giant's blood with the blood of the daughters of men. This was Satan's attempt to prevent the prophetic word in Genesis 3:15 that the seed of the woman would crush the head of the serpent, Satan.

We read further in Genesis that Noah built an Ark as instructed by the Lord for himself and his wife together with his sons and their wives. He was instructed by God exactly how many of which type of animal he should take into the Ark.

132

And then…it began to rain…the fountains of the deep were broken up and the windows of Heaven were opened. There was rain upon the earth for forty days and forty nights, but the waters prevailed on the earth for one hundred and fifty days and the Bible says that everything that had breath in its nostrils died. The Ark was raised above the waters and those inside it were preserved from death by God.

The Bible says it so beautifully in Genesis 8:1: *"And God remembered Noah…"* The word "remember" in the Hebrew is "zakhar" which also means to, recall or reflect upon. Noah came to God's mind and He reflected upon him. It can also mean "to declare," perhaps God took such pleasure in the faith and obedience of Noah that He began to declare his praises. God did not only remember Noah, he also remembered those with him too, both man and beast and sent a wind, which began to blow and dry up the land.

> *He was reminding Noah of the preciousness of blood because in it was life and atoning power.*

Eventually, as we read in Genesis 8:16, God told Noah that He and those with him could leave the Ark and the first thing that Noah did was to build an altar unto the Lord.

Then he took of every clean beast and offered burnt offerings on the altar. This was an offering of consecration. Noah consecrated himself and his family and the land back to God.

"And the Lord smelled a sweet savour; and the Lord said in his heart, I will not again curse the ground any more for man's sake; for the imagination of man's heart is evil from his youth; neither will I again smite any more every thing living, as I have done.

While the earth remaineth, seedtime and harvest, and cold and heat, and summer and winter, and day and night shall not cease" (Genesis 8:21, 22).

This is the second covenant that God made with man as He smelled the offerings that Noah offered up to Him.

God's Covenant with Noah included the following:

1. God promised He would never again destroy every living creature on the earth with a flood, because man's heart was evil anyway. In Genesis 9:12-16, God says that He will put a bow in the sky as a sign of this covenant; it would cause Him to remember His covenant. Whenever we see the rainbow in the sky we can think about God's everlasting covenant and His faithfulness in keeping His promise.

"And God said, This is the token of the covenant which I make between me and you and every living creature that is with you, for perpetual generations: I do set my bow in the cloud, and it shall be for a token of a covenant between me and the earth. And it shall come to pass, when I bring a cloud over the earth, that the bow shall be seen in the cloud: And I will remember my covenant..." (Genesis 9:12-15a).

2. In the following verse God introduces meat into the diet of man.

"But flesh with the life thereof, which is the blood thereof, shall ye not eat" (Genesis 9:4).

God said that man could eat the flesh of an animal but could not eat the flesh while the blood was still in it. Man could not eat or drink blood because you are drinking the life of that animal and anyone who did would be cut off.

3. *"Whoso sheddeth man's blood, by man shall his blood be shed: for in the image of God made he man"* (Genesis 9:6).

God places great value on the blood of mankind because He made man in His image. Because of this man's blood was not to be shed; if it was shed it had to be paid for, blood for blood. He was reminding Noah of the preciousness of blood because in it was life and atoning power. The world that had just been destroyed, out of which Noah had come, had been a world of violence, this was a reminder that murder was not permitted.

CHAPTER

6

THE BLOOD COVENANT

*T*he Bible is a book of Covenants. The Old Testament is really the Old Covenant. The New Testament is really the New Covenant in the Blood of Christ.

The word for covenant in Hebrew is "berith." It means, determination, stipulation, covenant.

The Greek word is "diatheke," which means to "cut covenant" with the idea that a covenant is made by the shedding of blood. In ancient Greek it also meant "testament" as in last will and testament, which is the record of the declarations and distribution of property after the death of the testator.

A covenant is a sacred contract that cannot be broken. It involved signs and blood sacrifices with the relationship being sealed in that blood with a solemn binding oath, which promised blessings if kept and curses if broken. Blood is what maintains life and carries the life of that person within it and it is taken to every cell of the body to bring life to that cell. When a Blood Covenant is cut, every cell of one's body is involved, every part of one's life so that there is not one area that is not sealed by the oath of the covenant. As the covenant is sealed with blood each of the covenant partners has literally given his life to the other.

> *When a Blood Covenant is cut, every cell of one's body is involved, every part of one's life so that there is not one area that is not sealed by the oath of the covenant.*

Many of the nations know about blood covenants instinctively because God has put it in their hearts. Instinctively they know that their blood represents their life and when they give their blood to another they give their lives. God has placed the secrets of eternity in the hearts of the people in nations that have never heard of Christ, just waiting for the time when someone would come and preach about the New Covenant in His Blood, so that they would understand. We who have lived in civilization have lost these important truths.

THE HEBREW BLOOD COVENANT

There are nine steps to the Hebrew Blood Covenant, which are important for us to understand if we are to receive all that we have been given through the shed Blood of Christ.

1. **The exchange of coats and robes.** The coat and robe represented everything that the person was. It was his authority, his stature, everything that he stood for. He was saying, "I give you everything that I am." It was his covering! What we wear represents us. A queen dresses like a queen. When we look at her we understand that she has the value systems of royalty, the wealth of royalty and

what stands behind her is a history of kings and queens who have lived in varying degrees of her stature, and she is standing in the full authority of what her throne represents.

2. **The exchange of belts.** The belt held their armor together. When they took their belt off they made themselves vulnerable to one another in that moment. The dagger, the sword, the bow and arrow were all held in place by the belt. When the belt was given, the person was vowing to protect his covenant partner, to lay down his life for him. He was saying, "This belt has saved my life and now I am giving it to you, the belt represents my defense and I will defend your life with the same diligence that I have defended my own. Whoever sees you from this moment on sees me standing behind you to fight for you." From that moment on he would not fight his battles alone, whoever fought one, would have to fight the other covenant partner too.

From that moment on he would not fight his battles alone, whoever fought one, would have to fight the other covenant partner too.

3. **Cut the Covenant.** When the covenant was cut, an animal was cut entirely down the middle and that included cutting through the head. The spine was cut through until there were two equal pieces lying side-by-side making two walls of blood. The only time in the Bible when this was done was in the covenant ceremony. The men entering into covenant stood between the pieces of the animal with their backs to each other and walked a figure of eight around the pieces, ending up facing each other. They are saying that they are going through a death process where they are dying to themselves and entering into a process of rebirth. They are dying to

their old lives and their old ways and are starting a new walk with their covenant partner. The figure eight in Scripture speaks of new beginnings. A figure eight lying on its side is the symbol for eternity.

Each half of the animal represented one covenant partner. In essence they are saying, "Let the Lord do the same to me as has happened to this animal if I break this sacred covenant." The only way out of the covenant was to die.

4. **Intermingling of blood.** The right arm is held up, the palms cut and then the hands are clasped together so that the blood intermingles. With the intermingling of blood came the intermingling of their lives. In other words, "Your life is as my life and my life as your life." Through the exchange of blood came the exchange of natures, "I am in you and you are in me." A union of two people took place. The practice of shaking hands in today's societies, which in essence means, "I am at peace with you," came from this part of the covenant ritual.

> *Through the exchange of blood came the exchange of natures, "I am in you and you are in me."*

5. **Exchange of names.** The one would take the other's last name and put it in the middle of their own name. When their names were heard it would be recognised that there was a change in their relationship and in their nature. They now had someone else to consider before themselves, they could not live as they used to, and there was someone that would consider them first, too.

6. **The Scar.** Through the cutting of the covenant a scar is formed which is the sign of being in covenant with someone. In some traditional cultures, herbs are put into this scar so that it stands out. The scar is the "seal" of a covenant. When the right arm

is held up so that an attacker sees the scar, the attacker knows that he is fighting more than one person and that person has a covenant partner who will come to his defense.

7. **Terms of the Covenant.** The partners stand before witnesses and give their terms. It is the same as if the last will and testament is being read. "Everything that I have is yours, my finances, my houses, my family, and now everything that you owe is my responsibility as well." If the one got into trouble in any way the other would help without being asked – it was his responsibility.

8. **Covenant meal.** This was done as a memorial of the covenant. Bread and wine was used, the bread represented their flesh and the wine represented their blood. A loaf of bread was taken and broken in two and they fed it to one another, saying, "This is symbolic of my body and I am now putting myself into you." And again with the wine, "This is symbolic of my blood and I am now pouring it into you." There was an exchange of life and the two become one new man with a new nature.

9. **A memorial.** In order to remember the covenant a tree was planted which had been sprinkled with the blood of the animal. They were saying, "The blood-sprinkled tree and the scar will always be a testimony of our covenant." It was also a picture of new family roots and a new tree of life, new generations and a picture that each partner would gain from the fruit of this covenant.

All the descendants of the covenant partners were included in this covenant because they were "in the loins" of their fathers. When they come of age they could chose to remain or withdraw from it.

CHAPTER

7

DAVID & JONATHAN

There was a very unique and beautiful relationship between David and Jonathan. They could meet and communicate in a realm that was unusual. They were soul friends, sharing sensitivity and closeness that came because of the way God made them. There was perfect understanding and trust between them that went beyond the ties of family relationships because their hearts were open to each other. They needed to hide nothing; they knew they were safe with each other.

The following Scriptures describe what happened as Jonathan listened to David talking to King Saul, Jonathan's father. Jonathan's heart was touched and opened. This friendship, and the covenant between them that came out of it, was formed in God's own hands. David was chosen by God to take the throne that Jonathan should have inherited and in their covenant exchange together, Jonathan gave it to him as they shared everything they were and had. Giving away the throne was not Jonathan's intent but it was part of God's plan for David.

"And it came to pass, when he had made an end of speaking unto Saul, that the soul of Jonathan was knit with the soul of David, and Jonathan loved him as his own soul. And Saul took him that day, and would let him go no more home to his father's house. Then Jonathan and David made a covenant, because he loved him as his own soul. And Jonathan stripped himself of the robe that was upon him, and gave it to David, and his garments, even to his sword, and to his bow, and to his girdle. And David went out whithersoever Saul sent him, and behaved himself wisely: and Saul set him over the men of war, and he was accepted in the sight of all the people, and also in the sight of Saul's servants" (1 Samuel 18:1-5).

After the covenant exchange Jonathan's soul was knit with David's, they recognised likeness of spirit in each other so they opened up to each other. The covenant they made came out of their love for each other. In many ways they were similar, they were both warriors that fought for their nation against the Philistines. David found his counterpart in Jonathan, even though he was Saul's son. Their families were included in this covenant relationship; if David was killed Jonathan would take David's family as his own and visa versa.

There have been many that have tried to relate this relationship to their own, but the question is, what happens when the test comes, will the relationship still stand? Would you be willing to die for one another? Is it something that God put together in purity as He did this one? We know this was a pure relationship because the Scriptures say of David:

"And David behaved himself wisely in all his ways; and the Lord was with him" (1 Samuel 18:14).

David was more than a warrior, he was a lover of God and God paid him the most wonderful compliment, He said of him:

"*… I have found David the son of Jesse, a man after mine own heart, which shall fulfil all my will*" (Acts 13:22). God knew that David would do everything that He would ask of him!

Peter, when he spoke to the 3,000 on the Day of Pentecost said of David: "*For David speaketh concerning him, I foresaw the Lord always before my face, for he is on my right hand, that I should not be moved*" (Acts 2:25).

David was a man after God's heart because he kept his eyes always on God's face. He measured his life according to what he saw in God, and being always aware of God at his side, nothing could move him.

> *David measured his life according to what he saw in God, and being always aware of God at his side, nothing could move him.*

"*And it came to pass as they came, when David was returned from the slaughter of the Philistine, that the women came out of all cities of Israel, singing and dancing, to meet king Saul, with tabrets, with joy, and with instruments of music. And the women answered one another as they played, and said, Saul hath slain his thousands, and David his ten thousands. And Saul was very wroth, and the saying displeased him; and he said, They have ascribed unto David ten thousands, and to me they have ascribed but thousands: and what can he have more but the kingdom? And Saul eyed David from that day and forward*" (1 Samuel 18:6-9).

When Saul heard the women singing this song he felt threatened and became jealous of David, eventually trying to kill David by throwing a javelin at him. When Jonathan realised that his father's intent was to kill David, Jonathan warned him helping him to escape.

Jonathan, in contrast to his father, Saul, was never jealous of David. He even prophesied that David would be king over Israel.

"And he said unto him, Fear not: for the hand of Saul my father shall not find thee; and thou shalt be king over Israel, and I shall be next unto thee; and that also Saul my father knoweth" (1 Samuel 23:17).

David and Jonathan renewed their covenant by reaffirming their commitment not only to each other but to their descendants also.

"And thou shalt not only while yet I live shew me the kindness of the LORD, that I die not: But also thou shalt not cut off thy kindness from my house for ever: no, not when the LORD hath cut off the enemies of David every one from the face of the earth. So Jonathan made a covenant with the house of David, saying, Let the LORD even require it at the hand of David's enemies. And Jonathan caused David to swear again, because he loved him: for he loved him as he loved his own soul" (1 Samuel 20:14-17).

This was a strengthening of a covenant that they had already made. David, even though Saul pursued him relentlessly to kill him, never forgot his covenant with Jonathan, particularly that he would show the kindness of God to the House of Jonathan, which was Saul's House too, since Jonathan was Saul's son.

THE STORY OF MEPHIBOSHETH

Jonathan married and had a son called Mephibosheth. Mephibosheth was five years old when news of the death of his father, Jonathan, and grandfather Saul the King, came to the family and servants.

"And Jonathan, Saul's son, had a son that was lame of his feet. He was five years old when the tidings came of Saul and Jonathan out of Jezreel, and his nurse took him up, and fled: and it came to pass, as she made haste to flee, that he fell, and became lame. And his name was Mephibosheth" (2 Samuel 4:4).

The household was caught up in fear that David would come in and slaughter all of them. They must have heard such terrible things about him from Saul. As Mephibosheth's nurse picked him up and ran with him, he fell out of her arms and his feet were crushed so that he could not walk. His nurse grabbed him up and took him to Lo-debar where they went into hiding with the rest of his father and grandfather's household. Lo-debar means "place without pasture," it was a wilderness place in the Samaritan slums, a hiding place for outlaws.

Mephibosheth must have feared David greatly and spoken against him as the whole household was taught the worst about him. It was David's fault that he was living in these slums and not in a king's house. It was his fault that in their haste to flee his feet were crushed and now he could not walk. His name had been changed from Merib Baal which was, "destroyer of idols" or "overcoming idols," to Mephibosheth, meaning, "breathing shame." There was nothing about him that looked like a prince, he lived amongst thieves, robbers and the desperately poor. Shame caught in his throat as he tried to breathe, fear clung to him as he looked at his hopeless situation. Even worse than his dire surroundings was the fear that he would be found by King David. Kings in those days destroyed all the heirs of the kings whose thrones they took.

Then, one day, David remembered his covenant with Jonathan. David had promised to show the kindness of God to Jonathan's family. Perhaps David had touched his scar and remembered, perhaps he had seen it and was thinking of his dear friend, Jonathan, who had died, or perhaps it was the same God Who "reflected" on Noah that reminded him.

> *"And David said, Is there yet any that is left of the house of Saul, that I may shew him kindness for Jonathan's sake?"* (2 Samuel 9:1).

Ziba, formerly one of Saul's servants, told David about Mephibosheth and immediately David had him brought to his courts. Imagine what that trip must have been like for Mephibosheth. Why had Ziba betrayed him? He knew that his life was over. David would probably have him killed. When Mephibosheth finally reached David's courts he fell on his face before David in reverence.

Because of the blood covenant the one who had everything sought out the one who had nothing.

> *"And David said unto him, Fear not: for I will surely shew thee kindness for Jonathan thy father's sake, and will restore thee all the land of Saul thy father; and thou shalt eat bread at my table continually. And he (Mephibosheth) bowed himself, and said, What is thy servant, that thou shouldest look upon such a dead dog as I am?"* (2 Samuel 9:7-8).

By saying to Mephibosheth, "Fear not…" David gave him his life back. Instead of treating him as a "dead dog" he raised him up to eat at his table like one of his own sons. Where Mephibosheth lacked, David supplied from his own abundance. He restored to Mephibosheth all the land of Saul. Everything that Jonathan would have inherited was restored to his heirs. It was no longer lost to Mephibosheth. Not only did David restore what was lost to Mehpibosheth but also David promised Mephibosheth provision for all his life. Because of the covenant made with Jonathan, David covered him, restored his dignity to him and became his protector.

Because of the blood covenant the one who had everything, David, sought out Mephibosheth, the one who had nothing. Mephibosheth had to choose to accept what David was offering!

This is an incredible story of restoration because of covenant. David, the man after God's own heart showed us the heart of the Father towards us because of the covenant in His Son's Blood.

CHAPTER

ABRAHAM

"After these things the word of the Lord came unto Abram in a vision, saying, Fear not, Abram: I am thy shield, and thy exceeding great reward" (Genesis 15:1).

When Abram heard God say that, he knew God was talking about covenant. "Abram – here is my coat, my weapons of defense and everything I own including myself. I am your everything, not just now but in the future!"

God was looking for a union with Abram. He wanted to give Abram Himself.

"And Abram said, Lord God, what wilt thou give me, seeing I go childless, and the steward of my house is this Eliezer of Damascus? And Abram said, Behold, to me thou hast given no seed: and, lo, one born in my house is mine heir. And, behold, the word of the Lord came unto him, saying, This shall not be thine heir; but he that shall come forth out of thine own bowels

shall be thine heir. And he brought him forth abroad, and said, Look now toward heaven, and tell the stars, if thou be able to number them: and he said unto him, So shall thy seed be" (Genesis 15:2-5).

Abram zeroed in on one thing, the thing that was foremost on his heart and was his greatest complaint – he did not have a son and heir.

In essence God was saying to Abram, "Wait a minute, Abram, your vision is too small, you are only looking for one person, a son. Don't you know that if I am your reward, you have Me? And if you have Me, you have everything!" So, God took him to a "broad" place, somewhere where He could show him the large expanse of the sky so that he could see the big picture – one without limitations. Not only would he have an heir, God said, but also his descendents would be like the stars, unable to be counted.

"And he believed in the Lord; and he counted it to him for righteousness" (Genesis 15:6).

This scripture speaks volumes about the character of God. The mere fact that Abraham believed Him was enough to satisfy God that Abraham was righteous. It was, and is, what God was looking for, someone who would believe Him and trust Him. He knew Abram's heart and knew that Abram would believe Him.

It is the way we see God that reveals our own condition of heart because it is the filter of things like prejudice, mistrust, and our own bitterness of soul, that cause us to see God incorrectly and mistrust Him, because none of those things are in Him. If we trust Him, it means that we are seeing Him clearly and our faith in Him imputes righteousness to us.

Did God find in Abram what was lacking in Adam? Or, did Abram, by his faith in God, tap into the salvation that was not yet manifest on the earth through the Lamb slain from the foundation of the world? Only God knows the answer and He can talk to our individual hearts about this.

ABRAHAMIC COVENANT

"And he said unto him, I am the Lord that brought thee out of Ur of the Chaldees, to give thee this land to inherit it. And he said, Lord God, whereby shall I know that I shall inherit it? And he said unto him, Take me an heifer of three years old, and a she goat of three years old, and a ram of three years old, and a turtledove, and a young pigeon. And he took unto him all these, and divided them in the midst, and laid each piece one against another: but the birds divided he not. And when the fowls came down upon the carcases, Abram drove them away" (Genesis 15:7-9).

Abram, in obedience to the Word of the Lord, cut the animals in half right down the spinal cord and the head and laid the pieces out in half, ready to walk through the center. He had created two walls of blood. He knew what God was asking for. From the beginning of this conversation, God had shown him the direction He was taking. God was getting ready to enter into covenant with Abram and Abram was ready to give all of himself to God. He was not sure how this was all going to happen, but he believed God and in obedience got everything ready.

"And when the sun was going down, a deep sleep fell upon Abram; and, lo, an horror of great darkness fell upon him" (Genesis 15:12).

Because of the greatness of God's plan through Abram, He could not allow the participation in this covenant of anyone less than Himself, so He put Abram out in the Spirit. The word "horror" in this verse means, "fear, something which was to be dreaded." The awesome fear of the Lord came upon Abram so that he would have no doubt with Whom he was going into covenant. He was encountering the Living God.

> *There was nothing Abram could add to this covenant, God did it all! God entered into covenant with God.*

"For when God made promise to Abraham, because he could swear by no greater, he sware by himself, Saying, Surely blessing I will bless thee, and multiplying I will multiply thee. And so, after he had patiently endured, he obtained the promise. For men verily swear by the greater: and an oath for confirmation is to them an end of all strife. Wherein God, willing more abundantly to shew unto the heirs of promise the immutability of his counsel, confirmed it by an oath: That by two immutable things, in which it was impossible for God to lie, we might have a strong consolation, who have fled for refuge to lay hold upon the hope set before us" (Hebrews 6:13-18).

God, The Greater, had to swear by Himself, because there was no one higher to take an oath to, when God says something He can not go back on His word – He is incapable of lying. There was nothing that Abram could add to this covenant, God did it all!

"And it came to pass, that, when the sun went down, and it was dark, behold a smoking furnace, and a burning lamp that passed between those pieces" (Genesis 15:17).

Only Someone of God's own greatness and character could take Abram's place and say, "I will die for you and give you everything that I have." God entered into covenant with God.

Jesus in the book of Revelation is described as having *"feet like unto fine brass as if they burned in a furnace."* And *"his countenance was as the sun shineth in his strength."* This was the pre-incarnate Christ in His glory passing through the walls of Blood, standing in Abram's place covenanting with His Father.

Jesus said in John 8:56 *"Your father Abraham rejoiced to see my day: and he saw it, and was glad."*

This was the day of Christ that Abram rejoiced to see. Included in this covenant were all of Abram's seed because they were in him, they were in his loins when the covenant took place.

Name Change: Being in covenant required a name change for Abram, so the H in YHWH went into the center of Abram's name, becoming Abraham:

"Neither shall thy name any more be called Abram, but thy name shall be Abraham; for a father of many nations have I made thee" (Genesis 17:5).

His wife Sarai, as part of Abraham's family and the one through whom the promised heir would come also had a name change. Her name was changed to Sarah.

The Seal of the Covenant: *"This is my covenant, which ye shall keep, between me and you and thy seed after thee; Every man child among you shall be circumcised. And ye shall circumcise the flesh of your foreskin; and it shall be a token of the covenant betwixt me and you"* (Genesis 17:10-11).

ABRAHAM

Circumcision became the seal of the Abrahamic Covenant and was a sign that everything that Abraham reproduced would have the touch of God on it!

GOD PUTS ABRAHAM THROUGH A TEST

"And he said, Take now thy son, thine only son Isaac, whom thou lovest, and get thee into the land of Moriah; and offer him there for a burnt offering upon one of the mountains which I will tell thee of" (Genesis 22:2).

Abraham did not know that he was setting the scene for one of the most important types and shadows of the Word of God. He was enacting the time that would come when the Father, God Himself, would be laying His own beloved Son on the altar of sacrifice.

The Scripture says that Abraham rose up early in the morning; he immediately obeyed what God had asked of him and went towards the land of Moriah. He took with him two young men, his son and wood for the offering. On the third day of his journey he left his servants behind and went on with his son saying that they were going to go and "worship." This word, "worship" means to prostrate oneself, obeisance; it has the sense of submitting oneself in obedience to another.

> *Abraham did not know that he was setting the scene for one of the most important types and shadows of the Word of God.*

He laid the wood for the sacrifice on his son, Isaac, just as the cross was laid on Jesus, and they went into the mountains. But, there was just one problem; they did not have an animal to sacrifice. Abraham's answer to Isaac is so beautiful when Isaac asks about it.

153

"And Abraham said, My son, God will provide himself a lamb for a burnt offering: so they went both of them together" (Genesis 22:8).

Abraham was about to lose his cherished son, his son of promise, the one that God had spoken to him about, but he trusts! He knows that God will not go back on His promises nor His covenant with Abraham, after all he had God's name right in the center of his own to remind him of it every time someone spoke his name.

"God would provide Himself a Lamb." It was not only a statement of confidence in a God that could raise Isaac from the dead to keep the promise, but also it was a statement that brought together the timelessness of God in the Lamb slain from the foundation of the world and the Son of God being laid on a cross, a Lamb that was without blemish.

> *God provided a ram for sacrifice and Abraham was given back his son as one raised from the dead on that third day!*

"And they came to the place which God had told him of; and Abraham built an altar there, and laid the wood in order, and bound Isaac his son, and laid him on the altar upon the wood. And Abraham stretched forth his hand, and took the knife to slay his son" (Genesis 22:9-10).

This is the most amazing scripture because Abraham took up his knife to go through with what God had told him to do. He proved his absolute trust in God. Here was faith together with works!

"And the angel of the Lord called unto him out of heaven, and said, Abraham, Abraham: and he said, Here am I. And he said,

Lay not thine hand upon the lad, neither do thou any thing unto him: for now I know that thou fearest God, seeing thou hast not withheld thy son, thine only son from me. And Abraham lifted up his eyes, and looked, and behold behind him a ram caught in a thicket by his horns: and Abraham went and took the ram, and offered him up for a burnt offering in the stead of his son. And Abraham called the name of that place Jehovah-jireh: as it is said to this day, In the mount of the Lord it shall be seen" (Genesis 22:11-14).

> *God had to prove Abraham for our sakes and for the sake of the future generations that would come out of him.*

The Angel of the Lord called to him out of Heaven: "Stop! You passed the test, Abraham, now I know that you fear or revere Me, that you have a holy respect for Me." (My own translation!). Abraham must have realized that since he had no real contribution to his covenant with God, God was utterly in control of it all. He must have remembered well when the Holy Presence of God came on him and he went into a deep sleep. Who knows what understanding he had during that time of the events that happened and his revelation of the heart of God.

God provided a ram for the sacrifice and Abraham was given back his son as one raised from the dead on that third day! God required his obedience, he had to prove Abraham for our sakes and for the sake of the future generations that would come out of him, both the generations in the natural and the generations of the same faith. God required the sacrifice of that which was precious! Because he was willing to do it it was as though it was done.

"By faith Abraham, when he was tried, offered up Isaac: and he that had received the promises offered up his only begotten son, Of whom it was said, That in Isaac shall thy seed be called: Accounting that God was able to raise him up, even from the dead; from whence also he received him in a figure" (Hebrews 11:17-19).

ABRAHAM'S REWARD

"And the angel of the LORD called unto Abraham out of heaven the second time, And said, By myself have I sworn, saith the LORD, for because thou hast done this thing, and hast not withheld thy son, thine only son: That in blessing I will bless thee, and in multiplying I will multiply thy seed as the stars of the heaven and as the sand which is upon the sea shore; and thy seed shall possess the gate of his enemies; And in thy seed shall all the nations of the earth be blessed; because thou hast obeyed my voice" (Genesis 22:15-18).

- God would bless him and multiply his seed as the stars in the sky, the sand on the seashore.

- His seed would possess the gate of his enemies.

- Through his seed all the nations of the earth would be blessed.

The coming Messiah, the Saviour of the World, would be born out of Abraham's seed.

CHAPTER

THE PASSOVER

The children of Israel had been in Egypt for four hundred years and had been severely oppressed and suffered at the hands of the Egyptians. They had gone to Egypt during Joseph's time because of the famine in their own land. After Joseph died there arose Pharaohs that did not know Joseph. Pharaoh and the Egyptians feared the Children of Israel because they had increased so much in strength and numbers. In their distress the Children of Israel began to cry out to the Lord God of Israel for deliverance and God heard their cry!

Out of their midst God raised up a deliverer. At a time when the Pharaoh had ordered all the male babies born to be thrown into the waters of the Nile, out of the House of the Tribe of Levi, a son was born. His mother hid him for three months until she could hide him no more and then in an effort to save his life, she built him an "ark" out of bulrushes and floated him down the Nile with his sister keeping watch.

The baby was found by Pharaoh's daughter, who took him into her own household, and raised him as her son, and she called his name, Moses, which means, "drawn out of the water." God had heard the cry of His people and in Moses raised up a deliverer!

The beginning of the Book of Exodus is the story of how God raised Moses up, finally sending him and his brother, Aaron, to the Pharaoh with a message, "Let My people go!" Pharaoh broke promise after promise to release the Israelites and God sent plague after plague on the land in warning and judgment. Pharaoh had not recognized his adversary! It was not a man, Moses, but it was The Most High, the God of Israel that he was opposing.

As long as we stay hidden in Christ, we are safe from the Destroyer because Jesus was struck and the Blood shed from His wounds protects us.

The Bible says that God hardened Pharaoh's heart! One wonders why God did this. Was it to display His power to the Egyptians and to show them the powerlessness of their own gods, or to show His might and delivering power to His people to deliver them out of their slave mentality? They had been slaves for a long time and it had become their identity.

Finally, after nine plagues upon Egypt, God said to Moses and Aaron:

"Speak ye unto all the congregation of Israel, saying, In the tenth day of this month they shall take to them every man a lamb, according to the house of their fathers, a lamb for an house" (Exodus 12:3).

The lamb had to be a male in its first year, without blemish, either sheep or goat, selected out on the 10th day of Abib (Nisan), kept until the 14th so that they could keep it under observation to make sure there was no blemish. It was to be killed some time after noon on 14th probably around 3:00 p.m. and eaten after 6:00 p.m., which would have been the 15th day of Abib. Anything that was not eaten was to be burned.

"And they shall take of the blood, and strike it on the two side posts and on the upper door post of the houses, wherein they shall eat it" (Exodus 12:7).

"For I will pass through the land of Egypt this night, and will smite all the firstborn in the land of Egypt, both man and beast; and against all the gods of Egypt I will execute judgment: I am the Lord. And the blood shall be to you for a token upon the houses where ye are: and when I see the blood, I will pass over you, and the plague shall not be upon you to destroy you, when I smite the land of Egypt" (Exodus 12:12).

Jesus calls Himself, "The Door" in John's gospel. On this first Passover, the Lord tells the Children of Israel to strike the doorposts and the upper doorpost with blood from the lamb. *"Strike"* is the Hebrew word *"naga"* – to smite, beat, punish, to cause physical pain. It is a type and a shadow of the way that the "Door," Jesus Himself would be struck. They were also told not to go outside their door but stay within their house. As long as we stay hidden in Christ, we are safe from the Destroyer because Jesus was struck and the Blood shed from His wounds protects us. He was struck in His head (upper door post) and on His hands and feet and side (side door posts).

"And ye shall take a bunch of hyssop, and dip it in the blood that is in the bason, and strike the lintel and the two side posts with the blood that is in the bason; and none of you shall go out at the door of his house until the morning. For the Lord will pass through to smite the Egyptians; and when he seeth the blood upon the lintel, and on the two side posts, the Lord will pass over the door, and will not suffer the destroyer to come in unto your houses to smite you" (Exodus 12:22-23).

> *Jesus, the Passover Lamb, was examined by the Father for 33 years; every attitude, every motive, every heart's desire, and was found to be with out blemish.*

Hyssop was known by the ancient peoples to have a special medicinal power and was known as the "Holy Herb." It was used as a poultice to heal inflammation, bruises, lung infection and any manner of illnesses including epilepsy. The oil from the Hyssop leaves was known to be a cleanser of the body and all its afflictions. It was also believed by the ancients, long before this first Passover, that Hyssop would ward off any evil spirit sent for destruction.

They dipped the Hyssop in the Blood of the lamb and struck the lintel and door posts and as they did, very probably, some of the leaves would have been crushed to release the fragrant oil and the fragrance would have reminded the Israelites of its reputation for deliverance. Hyssop has another unusual quality, it has water within the stems and that water would have also oozed out on the doorposts and was a beautiful picture of the wounded side of Christ and the blood and the water that came pouring out. They were kept by the blood, the water and the oil. Jesus the Christ, the Saviour of the world, the water of the Living Word of God brought together by the Precious Holy Spirit.

David refers to Hyssop when he says in Psalm 51:7: *"Purge me with Hyssop and I shall be clean."*

They ate the lamb in the night, a lamb for a household. They ate it with unleavened bread because there was no time for the bread to rise, and with bitter herbs, a sign of the bitterness of their bondage in Egypt. They had to eat fully clothed, with their shoes on and ready to go! The Israelites knew that blood was for atonement for sin, now they were going to see its mighty delivering power, but they had to obey God's instructions or the blood had no power to save them. They had to stay hidden within the house!

Now, not only were they hidden in the house, representative of being hidden in Christ, but also each one of them had eaten of the lamb and the lamb (Christ) was now inside them. As the Israelites left Israel they left as people that had all partaken of the lamb. The precious little lamb had to die so that their firstborn could live!

Later this sacrifice was to be the beginning of all sacrifices under the Mosaic Covenant.

JESUS IS THE PASSOVER LAMB

That which was precious had to be sacrificed!

Jesus, the Passover Lamb, was examined by the Father for 33 years; every attitude, every motive, every heart's desire, and was found to be without blemish. He was examined by the High Priests, He was examined by Pontius Pilot who said: *"...Ye have brought this man unto me, as one that perverteth the people: and, behold, I, having examined him before you, have found no fault in this man touching those things whereof ye accuse him"* (Luke 23:14).

"For we have not an high priest which cannot be touched with the feeling of our infirmities; but was in all points tempted like as we are, yet without sin" (Hebrews 4:15).

Jesus was fully God!

"And again, when he bringeth in the first begotten into the world, he saith, And let all the angels of God worship him" (Hebrews 1:6).

Jesus had to be tested as a man is to go beyond what He already was into perfection.

God said to His angels, "This is My Son! Worship Him!

When He was baptized of John, a voice came out of Heaven and said: *"Thou art my beloved Son; in thee I am well pleased"* (John 3:22c).

"For it became him, for whom are all things, and by whom are all things, in bringing many sons unto glory, to make the captain of their salvation perfect through sufferings" (Hebrews 2:10).

"...for Whom are all things" – God wanted an inheritance for His Son!

"...by Whom are all things" – In Whom everything has its existence!

The Amplified Bible says it this way:

162

"For it was an act worthy of God] and fitting [to the Divine Nature] the He, for Whose sake and by Whom all things have their existence, in bringing many sons into glory, should make the Pioneer of their salvation perfect [that is, should bring to maturity the human experience necessary for a perfect equipment for His Office as High Priest through suffering" (Hebrew 2:10).

Jesus had to be tested as man is to go beyond what He already was into perfection. He had to put on earth clothes and feel what we feel, undergo every temptation that we have ever undergone and stand perfect in overcoming power.

> *The Co-creator, One Who was already perfect became even more perfect.*

"Seeing then that we have a great high priest, that is passed into the heavens, Jesus the Son of God, let us hold fast our profession. For we have not an high priest which cannot be touched with the feeling of our infirmities; but was in all points tempted like as we are, yet without sin" (Hebrews 4:14).

There is a mystery in this! The Co-creator, One Who was already perfect became even more perfect. Nothing truly stands until it has been tested. Great declarations of love are nothing until they are tested. Friendship has to be tested, through all the slander, through all the trials of life will that friendship stand? Jesus said that greater love has no man than that he should lay down his life for a friend. The greatest love stands in the pathway of the bullet.

"Greater love hath no man than this, that a man lay down his life for his friends" (John 15:13).

THE BLOOD: ENTRANCE INTO THE SUPERNATURAL

These testings prove depth, the depth of love, the depth of friendship, the depth of relationship. It is all dimensional! Jesus was always "The Door." Even when He was slain from the foundation of the world, the Lamb without blemish, He was "The Door."

"And after six days Jesus taketh Peter, James, and John his brother, and bringeth them up into an high mountain apart, And was transfigured before them: and his face did shine as the sun, and his raiment was white as the light" (Matthew 17:2).

Jesus changed realms for a few minutes revealing Who He was. He revealed the Light of His Glory! He could have kept walking straight to His throne and sat down – but, He had an enemy to defeat, so He set His face as a flint!

> *His Blood and His broken body became the rent veil and the "The Way" into the Most Holy Place...*

"For the Lord GOD will help me; therefore shall I not be confounded: therefore have I set my face like a flint, and I know that I shall not be ashamed" (Isaiah 50:7).

His sufferings proved Him. The One Who already was "The Door" in Heaven, came to earth and lived in another dimension, and still proved to be perfect. He had gained victory in another dimension and became the doorway through the dimensions by which God could touch man and man could touch God. His Blood and His broken body became the rent veil and "The Way" into the Most

Holy Place, the Holy of Holies in the realms of Heaven. The place of the Glory!

"Having therefore, brethren, boldness to enter into the holiest by the blood of Jesus, By a new and living way, which he hath consecrated for us, through the veil, that is to say, his flesh" (Hebrews 10:19-20).

In the points below we see God's progression through three different men:

1. **Innocence:** Adam loved God in innocence. His trust in God was tested and did not stand.

2. **Righteousness:** Abraham was God's friend. His trust in God was tested. He believed God and it was counted to him as righteousness.

3. **Perfection:** Jesus was tested in every area and was perfected through His obedience.

10

THE COVENANT OF THE LAW OF MOSES

he Covenant of the Law (The Ten Commandments) was the Covenant God made with Moses. But, before this covenant there were certain ordinances that the Lord had given Moses so the people would have rules in order to live a higher, a more refined life.

These were people that came out of 400 years of enslavement and because of their struggles had forgotten how to behave toward their fellow man.

> *"And Moses came and told the people all the words of the Lord, and all the judgments: and all the people answered with one voice, and said, All the words which the Lord hath said will we do"* (Exodus 24:3).

The Israelites made an astounding declaration, *"Whatever God says we will do it!"* They did not realise that in saying that they had already set themselves under the law. The laws and ordinances of God require perfection. God was about to give them the Ten Commandments, the Law was never given to be kept because it was impossible for any human being to keep! It would have been much better for them to say, "God, we want to do everything you say but we know we are weak, so help us, give us your grace, and forgive us when we mess up because we know we will."

He was saying that His standards of absolute perfection are so high that there is no way mankind can accomplish it.

In essence what the Israelites were saying was, "We will be like God – because only God can keep the law."

"For whosoever shall keep the whole law, and yet offend in one point, he is guilty of all" (James 2:10).

The Law was given as God's standard of perfection. It could not only be obeyed in part, every single area, "every jot and tittle," had to be kept. If one tiny part was broken, all of it was broken. It was a mirror to show mankind our sin.

"Wherefore the law was our schoolmaster to bring us unto Christ, that we might be justified by faith" (Galatians 3:24).

"What shall we say then? Is the law sin? God forbid. Nay, I had not known sin, but by the law: for I had not known lust, except the law had said, Thou shalt not covet" (Romans 7:7).

Even if one kept the entire law there was one little problem in the tenth commandment, which was, *"Thou shalt not covet!"* This last commandment dealt with lust, and the intent and covetous desires of our hearts and that it would break the whole Law. If one only thought about the act of sin, the Law was broken! If a man only thought about his neighbour's wife incorrectly, it was as though he had committed the act in his heart. The Law pointed this out and so did Jesus in Matthew 5:28 in His Sermon on the Mount.

> *"For if they which are of the law be heirs, faith is made void, and the promise made of none effect: Because the law worketh wrath: for where no law is, there is no transgression. Therefore it is of faith, that it might be by grace; to the end the promise might be sure to all the seed; not to that only which is of the law, but to that also which is of the faith of Abraham; who is the father of us all"* (Hebrew 4:14-16).

Where there was no Law, there was no transgression! But now, the Law pointed out everyone's failings.

When the Law was broken it required the penalty of death! The only way to be released from the Law was not to try and adhere to it, but the penalty of death had to be paid. God was speaking loud and clear through the Law. He was saying that His standards of absolute perfection are so high that there is no way mankind can accomplish it.

...we were never created to live under hard rules. We were created for love and we were created for grace and truth.

The Israelites must have thought, "It was bad enough before, but now we have this standard that is hanging over our heads. It makes everything worse, we get into trouble just because of our thoughts!"

But, the Law was a Schoolmaster to show mankind that we are unable to fulfil the Law and be righteous. We needed a Saviour and one that could save us once and for all!

Every aspect of WHO HE WAS when He satisfied the Law affected His blood, because His Life is in His Blood.

Every time they thought a wrong thought they came under the curse of the Law. Any religious laws that we put ourselves under have the same effect. We think that we can do it, but the more we try the harder it gets and the more frustrated we get, because we were never created to live under hard rules. We were created for love, and we were created for grace and truth. The truth is that it is only by grace that we are saved, saved from hell and saved from religious rules! The Blood of Christ cries, "Mercy!"

"For Christ is the end of the law for righteousness to every one that believeth" (Romans 10:4).

"End" in Greek is *"telos"* (5056) reaching the goal, the place at which something ceases to be what it was, the point at which all previous activities cease.

"Christ hath redeemed us from the curse of the law, being made a curse for us: for it is written, Cursed is every one that hangeth on a tree" (Galatians 3:13).

Jesus' life fulfilled every aspect of the Law for us and His death on a tree (the cross) broke every curse. He was the final sacrifice for those who believe!

Every aspect of WHO HE WAS when He satisfied the Law affected His Blood, because His Life is in His Blood.

- Not only the power of an endless life

- Not only coming out of the species that is God

- But walking out every jot and tittle of the Law, so that not even one thought was out of line – the Law was utterly satisfied, utterly fulfilled.

We were IN Him when He died on the cross. When He died we died. When He rose up from the dead so did we! Condemnation and guilt were paid for – they are some of our enemies that were on the cross. They were part of the law when it had power over us, but they died with us when we were crucified and died with Christ.

The POWER of sin was broken off us so that we could walk in Holiness – just as He did. We were restored to a higher place. We may still struggle, but the power of every sin has been broken, we just have to know it!

"For the law of the Spirit of life in Christ Jesus hath made me free from the law of sin and death. For what the law could not do, in that it was weak through the flesh, God sending his own Son in the likeness of sinful flesh, and for sin, condemned sin in the flesh: That the righteousness of the law might be fulfilled in us, who walk not after the flesh, but after the Spirit" (Romans 8:2-4).

"Death is swallowed up in victory. O death, where is thy sting? O grave where is thy victory? The sting of death is sin; and the strength of sin is the law. But thanks be to God, which giveth us the victory through our Lord Jesus Christ" (1 Corinthians 15:54c-57).

When sin and death were still Law they had a power that could be wielded over our lives; the need for them to reign over us was totally satisfied. The power of sin and death have been silenced. Their legal document against us has been signed in the Blood of the Lamb, "Paid in Full!"

THE DAY OF ATONEMENT

This was the most solemn of all days for the Israelites. It is also called "Yom Kippur" the Day of Forgiveness, or the Day of Covering. It is held in our months of September-October or the 10th of Tishri, the seventh month of the Jewish calendar.

The power of sin and death has been silenced. Their legal document against us has been signed in the Blood of the Lamb,

"Paid in Full!"

Leviticus Chapter 16 should be read carefully. It has a detailed account of the ceremonial process expected of the High Priest, who was Aaron at that time. It is the only day of the year that the High Priest could enter into the Most Holy Place or Holy of Holies. He had to make atonement for himself before he could make atonement for the nation. It was a "Sabbath" religious holiday in which, although the people did not actively participate, they had to stay home, fast and consider their sins of the last year. This was the only chance in the whole year to get totally clean; they did not want to forget anything!

During this time of the first Day of Atonement, the people must have been in awe of God. The holy fear of the Lord must have been upon all the people because the two priestly sons of Aaron, Nadab and Abihu, had recently been struck down by God for presenting "strange fire" to Him.

The Shekinah Glory of God would appear as a cloud upon the Mercy Seat in The Most Holy Place, Aaron, the High Priest could not enter in carelessly lest he die. Because of this God gave Aaron very clear instructions how to enter in, what to do and what not to do.

The High Priest, as God's representative on the earth, would normally wear his beautifully brocaded clothing and jewellery, looking like a king, but on this occasion, after he had washed, he had to change and put on a set of linen clothes, which were very simple. Although these clothes were simple, the linen from which they were made came from Egypt, which was and still is the finest of linens. It came from the banks of the Nile and was called, Byssus (flax). The material made from this flax is very soft and very brilliantly white and was sold for twice its weight in gold.

Nobody could get into the presence of God without Blood.

God required linen because linen does not cause the body to sweat. Sweat represents work and there was no labour of man that could be added to the forgiveness of sins that God was about to extend to the nation. The Egyptian linen is brilliantly white beyond any other, signifying that the people's sins would be made "…white as snow!" Jesus' body was wrapped in linen when it was taken off the cross (John 19:40). Fine linen represents purity, holiness, and the righteousness of the saints. The Book of Revelation talks about the wife of the Lamb being arrayed in fine white linen

"...for the fine linen is the righteousness of saints" (Revelation 19:8c).

Aaron was to offer a young bullock in the Holy Place as a sin offering for himself and his family and offer a ram as a burnt offering. He would capture the blood of the bullock in a basin so that he could take it before the Lord. Then he would take two kids of goats and draw lots for them. One lot was the Lord's to be sacrificed, the other lot was for the scapegoat.

The Brazen Altar of the Tabernacle of Moses was the altar of Sacrifice where the blood of animals was shed and then poured out at the base of the altar. The Brazen Altar was at the entrance to the Tabernacle. Nobody could get into the Presence of God without Blood.

He would also have to take a censer full of hot coals off the altar and a handful of incense beaten very small and take them within the veil (Leviticus 16:12-13). Once inside the veil Aaron was to put the incense on the fire so that the smoke from the incense would cover the Mercy Seat and he would not die.

The sprinkling in front of the mercy seat represented the seven times that Jesus was struck and His Blood released...

The incense was considered holy and a symbol of the prayers and intercessions of the people rising before the Lord as a sweet fragrance. Another very important reason for the incense is that it would create a smoke screen to dim the brightness of the Glory so that Aaron would not die when he looked upon it.

Once that was done, the blood from the bullock for Aaron and his family was sprinkled on the Mercy Seat and in front of the

Mercy Seat, sprinkling it seven times with his finger. The sprinkling in front of the Mercy Seat represented the seven times that Jesus was struck and His Blood released, on His head, His side, His back, on both feet and on both hands.

Then Aaron would offer the Lord's goat as a sin sacrifice. The blood of this offering would be collected too and taken within the veil to the Mercy Seat, sprinkled on the Mercy Seat and then seven times with Aaron's finger before the Mercy Seat, this was done to cleanse the tabernacle for the accumulated uncleanness of the people during the year and for the sins of the people themselves.

He had to do this alone with nobody else around and he had to remain standing while within the veil, inside the Most Holy Place. He had to stand because that signified the unfinished work of this atonement. It had to be repeated every year because they were only restored to right standing before God for the past. They never changed and their consciences were never purged of sin! So Aaron had to stand!

"Which was a figure for the time then present, in which were offered both gifts and sacrifices, that could not make him that did the service perfect, as pertaining to the conscience" (Hebrews 9:9).

When he had done all of that, he could take the second goat, the one for the people, the scapegoat, he not only lay his hands upon it, he leaned on it and imparted the sins of the people onto the goat. It would be taken into the wilderness and let loose never to return. Signifying in this way that their sins were cast away as far as the east is from the west, never to be remembered again. They were restored to innocence but they could never move on to perfection.

Then the offerings from which blood was taken for the atonement would be taken outside the camp and burned.

A life for a life! Blood used to cleanse. All the sins of the people placed on a substitute!

The picture had been painted until the day that the temporary substitute was to be replaced with the eternal!

"Neither by the blood of goats and calves, but by his own blood he entered in once into the holy place, having obtained eternal redemption for us. For if the blood of bulls and of goats, and the ashes of an heifer sprinkling the unclean, sanctifieth to the purifying of the flesh" (Hebrews 9:12-13).

"But now hath he obtained a more excellent ministry, by how much also he is the mediator of a better covenant, which was established upon better promises. For if that first covenant had been faultless, then should no place have been sought for the second" (Hebrews 8:6).

JESUS WAS THE MEDIATOR OF THE NEW COVENANT

W hat is a "Mediator"? The word "Mesites" in the Greek means, one who stands between two parties to bring them into a place of peace with each other. Jesus is the Mediator between God and us. He came down and cut Covenant with us in His Blood. As God He came down to our level, put on human flesh, and met with us. Jesus, The Christ, the Anointed One, stepped into the place of the High Priest and carries us on His heart before the Father continually. He brings peace between the Father and us.

> *"Surely he hath borne our griefs, and carried our sorrows: yet we did esteem him stricken, smitten of God, and afflicted. But he was wounded for our transgressions, he was bruised for our iniquities: the chastisement of our peace was upon him; and with his stripes we are healed"* (Isaiah 53:4-5).

The Brazen Altar of the Tabernacle of Moses was the Altar of Sacrifice where the blood of animals was shed and then poured out at the base of the altar. The Brazen Altar was at the entrance to the Tabernacle, one could not get into the Presence of God without blood. This altar was made of brass and represented the judgment of God.

The cross became that altar. This is where our New Covenant was cut in His Blood. We were IN Him on the cross making covenant with God Who had laid all our sins upon Jesus. His Blood covered the cross and was poured out at the base of the cross. If we can receive the revelation that we died there, it will change our lives because then we can live in true resurrection power!

"Jesus, when he had cried again with a loud voice, yielded up the ghost. And, behold, the veil of the temple was rent in twain from the top to the bottom; and the earth did quake, and the rocks rent" (Matthew 27:50-51).

The veil in the temple separated the Most Holy Place or Holy of Holies, where God dwelt and where the Mercy Seat was, from the rest of the tabernacle. The Shekinah Glory, the settling Presence of God was in the Holy of Holies although at the time of the crucifixion the Ark had already been moved to the Tabernacle of David.

Jesus' flesh represented the veil, which hid God's glory. Within Him IS pure holiness, IS the Holy of Holies, IS the Shekinah Glory. His flesh was rent, like the veil in the temple, so that we may enter into the Presence of God, as we live hidden in Christ. The Holy of Holies represented the Throne Room of God.

"Let us therefore come boldly unto the throne of grace, that we may obtain mercy, and find grace to help in time of need" (Hebrews 4:16).

THE STEPS OF THE COVENANT

1. **He removed His robe.** In Psalms we read that God covers Himself in Light, Jesus is the "brightness of His glory" and the "express image" of His Person. He put aside His Heavenly ranking, His covering so after He had won us, He could share it with us. The Word became flesh and became of no reputation. The Adored One in Heaven, Who, with a word could command angels and universes, made Himself vulnerable and became one of us.

"And the Word was made flesh, and dwelt among us, (and we beheld his glory, the glory as of the only begotten of the Father,) full of grace and truth" (John 1:14).

He put aside His Heavenly ranking, His covering so after He won us, He could share it with us.

"Who, being in the form of God, thought it not robbery to be equal with God: But made himself of no reputation, and took upon him the form of a servant, and was made in the likeness of men" (Philippians 2:6-8).

2. **He took off His belt.** He walked away from everything that could have been a defense for Him and walked to the cross. The Hosts of Heaven, of whom He was Lord, were put on hold!

"Jesus answered, My kingdom is not of this world: if my kingdom were of this world, then would my servants fight, that I should not be delivered to the Jews: but now is my kingdom not from hence" (John 18:36).

178

3. **The covenant was cut in His Blood.** We walked through the bloody pieces of His body into covenant with God. The figure of eight represents newness of life. On its side, it is also the sign for eternity. The Diatheke – the Covenant of the Greater giving to the Lesser.

"And he said unto them, This is my blood of the new testament, which is shed for many" (Mark 14:24).

"And to Jesus the mediator of the new covenant, and to the blood of sprinkling, that speaketh better things than that of Abel" (Hebrews 12:24).

4. **Blood was shed.** He raised His arms so that His wrists could be wounded by crucifixion…the Blood poured out. Blood mingled with water came from His side.

"But one of the soldiers with a spear pierced his side, and forthwith came there out blood and water" (John 19:34).

5. **Exchange of names.** He gave us His name, Christ-ians – anointed ones or people of His light.

"And the disciples were called Christians first in Antioch" (Acts 11:26).

"Him that overcometh will I make a pillar in the temple of my God, and he shall go no more out: and I will write upon him the name of my God, and the name of the city of my God, which is new Jerusalem, which cometh down out of heaven from my God: and I will write upon him my new name" (Revelation 3:12).

6. **Make a Scar.** The scars were formed by the marks of the crucifixion, which remain for eternity.

"Then saith he to Thomas, Reach hither thy finger, and behold my hands; and reach hither thy hand, and thrust it into my side: and be not faithless, but believing. And Thomas answered and said unto him, My Lord and my God. Jesus saith unto him, Thomas, because thou hast seen me, thou hast believed: blessed are they that have not seen, and yet have believed" (John 20:27-30).

7. **Terms of the Covenant.** He has written His laws upon our hearts and we have become His people and He has become our God. Every provision that He has is abundantly available to us, whether health, wisdom, finances or the supply for any other kind of lack.

"For this is the covenant that I will make with the house of Israel after those days, saith the Lord; I will put my laws into their mind, and write them in their hearts: and I will be to them a God, and they shall be to me a people" (Hebrew 8:10).

8. **Covenant meal.** We remember our covenant with Him every time we break bread and drink of the cup of wine. We commune, have true fellowship with Him in this covenant meal and through it we have access to every need.

"Then Jesus said unto them, Verily, verily, I say unto you, Except ye eat the flesh of the Son of man, and drink his blood, ye have no life in you. Whoso eateth my flesh, and drinketh my blood, hath eternal life; and I will raise him up at the last day. For my flesh is meat indeed, and my blood is drink indeed. He that eateth my flesh, and drinketh my blood, dwelleth in me, and I in him. As the living Father hath sent me, and I live by the

Father: so he that eateth me, even he shall live by me. This is that bread which came down from heaven: not as your fathers did eat manna, and are dead: he that eateth of this bread shall live for ever" (John 6:53-56).

The cross was a tree planted and through it Jesus has become our covenant Tree of Life!

"And he took bread, and gave thanks, and brake it, and gave unto them, saying, This is my body which is given for you: this do in remembrance of me. Likewise also the cup after supper, saying, This cup is the new testament in my blood, which is shed for you" (Luke 22:19-20).

9. **A memorial** in which a blood sprinkled tree was planted. Once Jesus was on the cross, it was lifted up and dropped into the hole made for its support. It was a tree planted and through it Jesus has become our covenant Tree of Life!

"And we are witnesses of all things which he did both in the land of the Jews, and in Jerusalem; whom they slew and hanged on a tree" (Acts 10:39).

BLOOD ON THE MERCY SEAT

The blood of sacrifice had to be sprinkled on the Mercy Seat, which was the lid of the Ark of the Covenant and was made of pure gold. The Ark of the Covenant was within the Most Holy Place.

The Hebrew word for the lid of the Ark of the Covenant is, "Kaporet" meaning, "atonement piece." It is probably taken from the word, "kaphar" which literally means, "wipe out." This implies that "Kaporet" means "thing of wiping out or thing of cleansing."

The Greek word for Mercy Seat, "hilasterion" literally means "propitiation" or the gift that procures mercy through God's indignation being satisfied.

Athough both the translations from the Hebrew and the Greek words is not directly, "Mercy Seat" that is what it is in function. The term "Mercy Seat" is believed to have been translated from the German word, "gnadenstuhl" meaning "seat of grace" or "the location of grace."

Only the Blood of Christ could cleanse the Mercy Seat in Heaven...

"It was therefore necessary that the patterns of things in the heavens should be purified with these; but the heavenly things themselves with better sacrifices than these. For Christ is not entered into the holy places made with hands, which are the figures of the true; but into heaven itself, now to appear in the presence of God for us" (Hebrews 9:23-24).

The Tabernacle of Moses was only a picture or a pattern on earth of the real Tabernacle in Heaven. Only the Blood of Christ could cleanse the Mercy Seat in Heaven and that is where it lives eternally.

"Who being the brightness of his glory, and the express image of his person, and upholding all things by the word of his power, when he had by himself purged our sins, sat down on the right hand of the Majesty on high" (Hebrews 1:3).

Paul in Romans 3:25, declares that Christ Jesus is the true Mercy Seat and He was covered with His own Blood. He is the propitiation, the means by which God's wrath was satisfied. The ultimate and final offering!

> *"Whom God hath set forth to be a propitiation through faith in his blood, to declare his righteousness for the remission of sins that are past, through the forbearance of God"* (Romans 3:25).

When Christ had done all of these things and completed His High Priestly atoning work, He **sat down** at the right hand of the Father signifying that there was no need for any other atonement – it was finished! Aaron, as High Priest and all the others after him, could never sit down in the Holy of Holies, they had to stand or die, because every year they had to offer the same offerings. But, Christ did it once for all, and sat down as the Christ in the Throne Room of Heaven of which the Holy of Holies was a picture!

> *"For such an high priest became us, who is holy, harmless, undefiled, separate from sinners, and made higher than the heavens; Who needeth not daily, as those high priests, to offer up sacrifice, first for his own sins, and then for the people's: for this he did once, when he offered up himself"* (Hebrews 7:26-27).

> *"If ye then be risen with Christ, seek those things which are above, where Christ sitteth on the right hand of God. Set your affection on things above, not on things on the earth. For ye are dead, and your life is hid with Christ in God. When Christ, who is our life, shall appear, then shall ye also appear with him in glory"* (Colossians 3:1-4).

And now, as our High Priest, He ever lives to make intercession for us.

"Wherefore he is able also to save them to the uttermost that come unto God by him, seeing he ever liveth to make intercession for them" (Hebrews 7:25).

"Who is he that condemneth? It is Christ that died, yea rather, that is risen again, who is even at the right hand of God, who also maketh intercession for us" (Romans 8:34).

THE BLOOD OPENS THE WAY FOR US TO SEE GOD

"And he sent young men of the children of Israel, which offered burnt offerings, and sacrificed peace offerings of oxen unto the Lord. And Moses took half of the blood, and put it in basons; and half of the blood he sprinkled on the altar. And he took the book of the covenant, and read in the audience of the people: and they said, All that the Lord hath said will we do, and be obedient. And Moses took the blood, and sprinkled it on the people, and said, Behold the blood of the covenant, which the Lord hath made with you concerning all these words" (Exodus 24:5-8).

> *After the blood was sprinkled, the people saw God on His Throne...*
>
> *God delights to reveal Himself to us, to show us His glory...*

Moses sprinkled the blood on the altar.

Then he sprinkled the people.

"Then went up Moses, and Aaron, Nadab, and Abihu, and seventy of the elders of Israel: And they saw the God of Israel: and there was under his feet as it were a paved work of a sapphire

184

stone, and as it were the body of heaven in his clearness. And upon the nobles of the children of Israel he laid not his hand: also they saw God, and did eat and drink" (Exodus 24:9-11).

After the blood was sprinkled, the people saw God on His Throne and they did not die.

God delights to reveal Himself to us, to show us His glory, His majesty and most of all to find a meeting place with us where we can commune with Him.

GOD DID IT ALL!

"For this is the covenant that I will make with the house of Israel after those days, saith the Lord; I will put my laws into their mind, and write them in their hearts: and I will be to them a God, and they shall be to me a people" (Hebrews 8:10).

We, as God's Covenant people, are no longer under a set of rules but God covenanted with Himself to write His laws in our hearts so that we would "want to" be like Him and doing His will would be "normal" life to us.

"Can two walk together, except they be agreed?" (Amos 3:3).

CHAPTER

12

THE CRUCIFIXION OF JESUS

The crucifixion is unanimously regarded as the cruelest, most horrible form of execution reserved only for the vilest of criminals. Among the Romans, degradation was part of the torment, and so, the victim was stripped naked of all his clothing. The anticipation of the intense cruelty and suffering to come must have been terrible for the victim.

The following scriptures describe the crucifixion of Jesus:

Matthew 26:57 – 27:56

Mark 14:53 – 15:41

Luke 22:66 – 23:49

John 18:12 – 19:37

1. The Scourging: Jesus was taken to the Court of the Pavement where the Romans had a scourging post, which had a steel ring at the top. The rope that tied His hands was put through the ring and He was pulled up so that His arms were stretched out and He was

on His tiptoes. In this way His skin on His back and body would be stretched tight. His robe was ripped off to expose bare skin.

The Scourge (*the flagellum*): This could have been a "cat o' nine tails" or could have had three tails attached to a handle and would have had bone, wood or broken pottery attached to the ends and sometimes part way up as well. The ends were dipped into sheep or goat blood, which served two purposes:

- The bacteria in the animal's blood would cause infection.

- The blood as it dried would become sticky and attach itself to the body of the victim, ripping off pieces of flesh as the whip was pulled back.

The one side of the victim was whipped until there was no sound flesh left and then they would move to the other side. The goal was to allow the victim's bowels to spill out onto the ground.

It was known to the Romans as the half-way death, 40 minus 1 lashes = 39.

2. They spat on Him, punched Him and mocked Him. They blindfolded Him and punched Him and demanded that He tell them who had done it.

"And the men that held Jesus mocked him, and smote him. And when they had blindfolded him, they struck him on the face, and asked him, saying, Prophesy, who is it that smote thee?" (Luke 22:64).

3. They dressed Him in a purple robe, put a scepter in His hands and a crown of thorns, probably shaped like a cap, on His head. The thorns would have been 5 – 6 inches long.

"And the soldiers platted a crown of thorns, and put it on his head, and they put on him a purple robe, And said, Hail, King of the Jews! and they smote him with their hands" (John 19:2-3).

"They plucked out the hair of his beard: I gave my back to the smiters, and my cheeks to them that plucked off the hair: I hid not my face from shame and spitting" (Isaiah 50:6).

4.   He was taken before Pontius Pilate and suffered the betrayal of many of whom He had loved and ministered to, who cried out, "Crucify Him!" and then they chose Barabbas, who was a criminal.

"But the chief priests and elders persuaded the multitude that they should ask Barabbas, and destroy Jesus. The governor answered and said unto them, Whether of the twain will ye that I release unto you? They said, Barabbas. Pilate saith unto them, What shall I do then with Jesus which is called Christ? They all say unto him, Let him be crucified" (Matthew 27:20-22).

The cross was lifted up and dropped into the ground causing intense pain as His whole body shook with the impact of it

5. A cross beam (weighing about 125 lbs) was put across His shoulders and He was made to walk up the Via Dolorosa to Golgotha. It is a very steep road. He fell beneath the weight of it. Simon of Cyrene picked it up and carried it for Him.

"And they compel one Simon a Cyrenian, who passed by, coming out of the country, the father of Alexander and Rufus, to bear his cross" (Mark 15:21).

6. At Golgotha He was laid on the cross with hands outstretched and into each wrist was hammered an 8 inch nail which went between the small bones, bursting open arteries and other blood vessels and hit the ulnar nerve causing the thumb to move towards the palm.

7. His feet were overlapped sole to instep, both feet extended straight down and a 12-inch spike was driven through His instep coming out through the heel of the lower foot and into the wood of the cross.

8. Fastened to the top of the cross was the *titulus* which was an inscription written on wood stating the victim's name and crime.

The cross was kept close to the ground so that anyone who wanted could go up and beat the victim on the cross.

"*And set up over his head his accusation written, THIS IS JESUS THE KING OF THE JEWS*" (Matthew 27:37).

9. The cross was lifted up and dropped into the ground causing intense pain as His whole body shook with the impact of it. The cross was kept close to the ground so that anyone who wanted could go up and beat the victim on the cross.

10. The pain of hanging on the cross would have been so intense that it would have gone down His arms into His chest and lungs causing massive spasms of the diaphragm so that He could not breathe. He would have to push His body weight up using His feet to get some breath and relieve the spasms in His chest.

189

11. Within the next three hours that He hung on the cross there would have been serum build up around the pericardium that surrounds the heart, which would have crushed His heart. The loss of body fluid would now have reached a critical stage and His compressed heart would be pumping out thick sluggish blood causing Him extreme thirst.

"After this, Jesus knowing that all things were now accomplished, that the scripture might be fulfilled, saith, I thirst" (John 19:28).

12. The victim's legs would be broken to ensure that they were dead. But, the scriptures say that not one bone of His body would be broken and in fulfillment of that prophecy the soldier pierced His side with a spear and blood mixed with water came out. One medical report says that for this to happen His heart must have ruptured; otherwise the fluid would have been contained within the thoracic cavity.

"But one of the soldiers with a spear pierced his side, and forthwith came there out blood and water. And he that saw it bare record, and his record is true: and he knoweth that he saith true, that ye might believe. For these things were done, that the scripture should be fulfilled, A bone of him shall not be broken. And again another scripture saith, They shall look on him whom they pierced" (John 19:34-37).

NEVERTHELESS – HE LIVES!

CHAPTER

THE OVERCOMING CHRIST

"And I heard a loud voice saying in heaven, Now is come salvation, and strength, and the kingdom of our God, and the power of his Christ: for the accuser of our brethren is cast down, which accused them before our God day and night. And they overcame him by the blood of the Lamb, and by the word of their testimony; and they loved not their lives unto the death" (Revelation 12:10, 11).

The Blood of the Lamb being shed brought down the Accuser of the brethren, who accused the brethren before God day and night. The "loud voice" in Heaven proclaimed four things that were "come" because of Him being brought down. Those things had "come!"

1. **Salvation.** The Greek word is, "Soteria," meaning deliverance in every way, both spiritually and physically, temporally (of earthly time) and eternally. Describing what the Saviour bestows including every blessing available. Every aspect of salvation has come!

2. Strength. Dunamis power. "Dunamis" means having received every capability from Christ, His strength and also His strength of will to do what is right and to choose the Father's will at all costs. Where we are weak He is strong in us. It is not the fact of our ability but the truth of His resurrection power in us. Dunamis power in us, the inherent ability to do everything that He did and walk in overcoming power, releasing signs, wonders and miracles on the earth. That strength has come!

3. The Kingdom of our God. The word used here is, "basileia" in the Greek, the area of jurisdiction of a King. It is taken from a word, "basis," meaning foundational support. As we entered into the *"Kingdom of His dear Son,"* which is a Kingdom of Light because Christ is Light, we are standing on the foundational support of His dominion authority and that authority coming through our mouths has the power to move mountains. Our place as intercessors standing in the authority of Christ on the earth comes from our position in the Heavens as we stand on the threshing floor of the stones of fire, the sapphire stones upon which God's Throne stands. It is a place won for us by the overcoming Christ. It is the place where we take up the baton from Him, where His mantle, which was dipped in His own Blood, was thrown to us. The mystery is that this incredibly powerful Kingdom is inside us. Will we take up the challenge for it is come!

> *...because Christ is Light, we are standing on the foundational support of His dominion authority and that authority coming through our mouths has the power to move mountains.*

4. The Power of His Christ. "Christos" means "anointed One," It would particularly have been used of one being anointed with oil to become the High Priest. The One Who is anointed to sit on the Thrones of the universe! "The Power" – the Greek word here is "exousia," which has its roots in the word, "exesti." This comes from two words, "ex" meaning "the point from which a motion or action proceeds," and "eimi" "to be or I AM." Christ is the point from which every motion or action proceeds. Exousia grants executive power directly from the Throne of One Who has always existed. It also means justified in having and exercising that power and the dominion of Divine Government. It is a combination of right and might. It is the authority of Christ that covers us with ability, power and strength. The Power of His Christ has come!

HIS OVERCOMING PEOPLE

1. They overcame by the Blood of the Lamb. Within the Blood of the Lamb is the power to overcome, it is like a blood transfusion into our blood vessels. His overcoming Life covers us and flows through us. It has been scientifically proven that blood transfusions can bring about a change in character because the LIFE of the person who gave the blood is in it. If we can only yield,

The Blood of Jesus has a Voice that cries out the victory reminding the demons of their defeat at Calvary!

we already have the power through His Blood, to become like Him.

It is also a weapon that will stop the enemy in their tracks; they cannot pass through the Blood. The Blood of Jesus has a Voice that cries out the victory reminding the demons of their defeat at Calvary! There is no other voice like it – it spans eternity and it penetrates dimensions. When the angels hear the cry of a Blood-bought saint asking for the protection of the Blood, I believe they are alerted and quickly gather to that place.

The Blood of Jesus is precious in Heaven – every drop of it is PURE LOVE!

2. **They overcame by the Word of their Testimony.** The word for testimony in the Greek is the word from which we take "martyr," "marturomai" or "to be called in as a witness." We are living testimonies of what Christ has done in our lives and as we speak about it we release the power of it into the lives of others. We are living examples, the truth and reality of what we say has an anointing upon it! God has given us a voice that we should allow nobody to stop. Martyrs gave their lives because nothing would silence them. There is overcoming power in constantly testifying about what the Lord has done. There is overcoming power in constantly speaking His Word of victory.

> *Death is refusing to operate in the power of the soul to get our own way and the things we desire. It means taking the least place instead of the highest.*

3. **They overcame by loving not their lives unto the death.** This is the overcoming power of a broken will and a yielded life, someone who will do whatever God asks of them. Acknowledge that you have already been crucified with Christ. Nobody can take from you what you have died to. When we are faced with a death situation we can say, "We have already died!"

We have to give up the struggle to retain our lives. Take a step backwards in a power struggle and you will fall into the arms of Christ. I will always remember the anecdote that I read when I worked in the corporate world, where careers are often formed and made by climbing on another's shoulders or walking over people. "The problem with the Rat Race is that even the losers are Rats!" Death does not only mean going to the guillotine, it is refusing to operate in the power of the soul to get our own way and the things we desire. It means taking the least place instead of the highest.

"I am crucified with Christ: nevertheless I live; yet not I, but Christ liveth in me: and the life which I now live in the flesh I live by the faith of the Son of God, who loved me, and gave himself for me" (Galatians 2:20).

When Jesus died I was in Him. Everything I was died on that day.

In every life there has to be an altar on which the Precious is laid – every dream, every promise, every person precious to us has to die on that altar until the Spirit gives it life as He wills.

I bear in my body the mark of my covenant with God – a circumcised heart and the marks of the crucifixion.

In the Blood of Jesus is the ability to live the crucified life.

"Who, being in the form of God, thought it not robbery to be equal with God: [7] But made himself of no reputation, and took upon him the form of a servant, and was made in the likeness of men: And being found in fashion as a man, he humbled himself, and became obedient unto death, even the death of the cross" (Philippians 2:6-8).

The Amplified Bible puts it this way:

Who, although being essentially one with God and in the form of God [possessing the fullness of the attributes which make God God], did not think this equality with God was a thing to be eagerly grasped or retained; But stripped Himself [of all privileges and rightful dignity] so as to assume the guise of a servant (slave), in that He became like men and was born a human being. And after He had appeared in human form He abased and humbled Himself [still further] and carried His obedience to the extreme of death, even the death of the cross!

Because of all this He was exalted by God and given a name which is above every other name.

It was essential that He took this road because He was showing how to live.

Do not seek for position, or titles, nor to be highly thought of. Jesus did not hold on to His position as God, but took off His robe and put on that of a servant and knelt down to wash feet. He humbled Himself in obedience, but, that did not cause Him to lose His position in Heaven, it strengthened it. The Kingdom that we are an essential part of, The Kingdom of Heaven, is an everlasting Kingdom and has eternal values and we, as Sons of God, are strengthened by following His example of humility.

Do not seek for position, or titles, nor to be highly thought of.

Jesus did not hold on to His position as God, but took off His robe and put on that of a servant and knelt to wash feet.

"That I may know him, and the power of his resurrection, and the fellowship of his sufferings, being made conformable unto his death; If by any means I might attain unto the resurrection of the dead" (Philippians 3:10).

Our hearts cry is to know Him more. How? In the fellowship of His sufferings! But, to partake of this fellowship we have to know Him in the power of His resurrection or we will be overcome.

"Being made conformable" the Greek word is "summorphoo" (4833) – to assimilate. In other words, to be assimilated into His death is to be assimilated into His Resurrection, into His Life and power because He lives through us!

CHAPTER

14

PASSION FOR CHRIST

These are the last days of time as we know it! Many things are going to change and so we have to live in a state of constant change moving from glory to glory and allowing God to change our ideas and perceptions. The basic foundational principles of the Word of God will never change. But we, as people of the Spirit, must allow the Holy Spirit, to make any change that He wants to make in our lives. We should be eager for the Holy Spirit's input into our lives because He is preparing us for the time that is now upon us. Our greatest purpose in God is about to be revealed and we must co-operate with Him in the finest detail for the will and purpose of God to be made manifest upon the earth. We are here for Him! We live and breathe and move and have our being in Him, in Christ, Who is our All.

The culmination of all things is upon us and a release of the Glory is coming in a way such as we have never known or imagined. It is in being enmeshed with the Holy Spirit, in Divine Union with Him, that He can do His exploits. These are days of love and glory and war, but in it all we are seated in Heavenly places with Christ as Paul says in Ephesians 1:20. We must develop an intimate knowledge of Him in these days. We can know Him as the Lover of our souls in the Song of Solomon and the Glorious King of the Book of Revelation.

Passionate love will pursue Him until He reveals Himself.

"And in the midst of the seven candlesticks one like unto the Son of man, clothed with a garment down to the foot, and girt about the paps with a golden girdle. His head and his hairs were white like wool, as white as snow; and his eyes were as a flame of fire; And his feet like unto fine brass, as if they burned in a furnace; and his voice as the sound of many waters. And he had in his right hand seven stars: and out of his mouth went a sharp twoedged sword: and his countenance was as the sun shineth in his strength. And when I saw him, I fell at his feet as dead. And he laid his right hand upon me, saying unto me, Fear not; I am the first and the last: I am he that liveth, and was dead; and, behold, I am alive for evermore, Amen; and have the keys of hell and of death" (Revelation 1:13-17).

John, the Beloved, walked and lived with Jesus for three years. John knew Jesus' very heartbeat as John laid his head on Jesus' chest many times. John drew as close as could get many times and hung

Our greatest purpose in God is about to be revealed and we must co-operate with Him in the finest detail for the will and purpose of God to be made manifest upon the earth.

onto every word that Jesus spoke until those words transformed him. He was being prepared for the greatest revelation of all – to write a book beyond himself of a time he knew nothing about and could not even imagine the culture and technical advancement of these times. But, he had to bypass his own thinking, obey and write.

"Now there was leaning on Jesus' bosom one of his disciples, whom Jesus loved" (John 13:23).

When he saw the Christ described here in the Book of Revelation, even though he had known the man, Jesus, had seen Him on the Mount of Transfiguration, had stood by him when Jesus was crucified and had seen Him after His resurrection, this Christ caused him to fall down at His feet as a dead man. The Glory of His appearing overcame the natural strength of John's body and he was as one dead. Christ had to lay his right hand on him to strengthen him so that he could continue with the task at hand. I believe that John at that moment encountered the "Door" that transported him into a dimension that enabled him to write the Book of Revelation, but he had to pass through a "death" into a new realm of resurrection, "zoe" life, a new realm of Glory.

> *Wherever He walked His fire of purification would fall and that place would be weighed in the balance to see what would be left.*

Christ was wearing a stately robe down to His feet but His feet could be seen. They looked as though they were brass still molten in a burning furnace. The continual flowing within His feet of fire and molten brass is the picture of refining. Wherever He walked His fire of purification would fall and that place would be weighed in the balance to see what would be left. He is the measure and the plumb line.

He wore a golden girdle or belt around His breast possibly down to His waist. He was dressed to deliver a refining message to the churches. The Greek word for girdle, "zone" is akin to the word, "zugos" meaning to join especially by a yoke or a coupling, or being yoked to an obligation. It is also the word used for the balance beam on a scale, from the ends of which the scales themselves are hung. In other words, He is the pivotal point. He is the point of adjustment. He holds all things in balance.

John saw intense electrifying light around the head of Christ and His face, which was like looking into the sun. His face shone with His power and authority. His eyes revealed Who He is – a consuming fire! When He spoke His voice was as the sound of many waters because as He spoke not only words came out

> *He is the pivotal point.*
>
> *He is the point of adjustment.*
>
> *He holds all things in balance.*

but the intensity of vision; the impartation of what John needed to see and know. It was all compacted within the sound because it was from another realm and needed to unfold within John's spirit, which was also from that realm, and then interpreted into the language of earth. The authority by which Christ spoke was like a sword! John says that out of His mouth came a two-edged sword – it is hard for us to imagine what this must have looked like. The sound of His voice must have been powerful!

This is the Christ that we represent and that we know and love! We have nothing to fear. He is the One that revealed Himself to John and gave him the whole scenario of what He is going to do and what His enemies are going to do. Can you imagine a general in the military knowing every step of the enemies plan? There is no fear of that general losing the battle, He knows His enemy well.

This revelation of Christ should move us to passion for Him, inspire us to follow Him "whithersoever He goeth." It should draw us into His Presence as moths into a flame. He is only to be feared if we are watching at a distance, but close up the fire of His Glory causes us to burn for Him!

He was dead but now He is alive forever and what's more, He holds the keys of hell and death!

DANIEL'S VISION
OF THE PRE-INCARNATE CHRIST

Daniel, after he had been on a 21 day fast, saw the pre-incarnate Christ.

"Then I lifted up mine eyes, and looked, and behold a certain man clothed in linen, whose loins were girded with fine gold of Uphaz: His body also was like the beryl, and his face as the appearance of lightning, and his eyes as lamps of fire, and his arms and his feet like in colour to polished brass, and the voice of his words like the voice of a multitude" (Daniel 10:5-6).

The men with Daniel did not see this vision but "a great quaking fell upon them" and they ran away to hide. Daniel himself lost his strength and fell with his face on the ground as though he was in a deep sleep.

God is preparing an army of His Blood-bought saints that will enter into realms of the Spirit that are being opened up in this final hour. They will join with His Son, the One Who has given us just a glimpse of Who He is through His appearances to John and Daniel. He is the Victor in the final war between Light and Darkness. We already know which Kingdom wins. The questions is: How many will we take with us into the Kingdom of our God and of His Christ?

THE BLOOD OF THE LAMB

The Book of Revelation Chapter 5 describes so beautifully that the Lion of the Tribe of Judah had prevailed and was worthy to take the book out of God's hand and open up the seals, and then, in verse 6, John saw a Lamb, as it had been slain, and the Lamb came forward and took the book and opened the seals.

"And they sung a new song, saying, Thou art worthy to take the book, and to open the seals thereof: for thou wast slain, and hast redeemed us to God by thy blood out of every kindred, and tongue, and people, and nation; And hast made us unto our God kings and priests: and we shall reign on the earth" (Revelation 5:9-10).

Everything in our lives is preparing us to take this place of reigning for which the Lamb redeemed us.

The Lamb redeemed us to God by His Blood and then made us kings and priests unto God. That alone made Him worthy! Because of Him we shall reign on the earth. Everything in our lives is preparing us to take this place of reigning for which the Lamb redeemed us. Let us walk as kings and priests, as sons of the Most High God, sons that have no room in their lives for that which will bring disrepute to their Father!

"And one of the elders answered, saying unto me, What are these which are arrayed in white robes? and whence came they? And I said unto him, Sir, thou knowest. And he said to me, These are they which came out of great tribulation, and have washed their robes, and made them white in the blood of the Lamb" (Revelation 7:9-13).

"And I saw heaven opened, and behold a white horse; and he that sat upon him was called Faithful and True, and in righteousness he doth judge and make war. His eyes were as a flame of fire, and on his head were many crowns; and he had a name written, that no man knew, but he himself And he was clothed with a vesture dipped in blood: and his name is called The Word of God" (Revelation 19:13).

THE MORAVIANS

Following a revival among the Moravian people in 1727, a prayer meeting was formed of "hourly intercession." This prayer meeting lasted for a hundred years, 24-hour prayer, seven days a week. Their crest was the Lamb of God carrying a flag of victory which had a red cross on it. The motto encircling this crest said, "The Lamb has conquered, let us follow Him." The Moravians learned that the way to really love the souls of men was to first love, without reservation, the Saviour of men.

Missionaries, willing to risk their lives, went out from among the Moravians to the nations. One day, as two Dutch missionaries set out for the Dutch West Indies, they gave a great shout, which became the passionate call of the Moravians:

"May the Lamb that was slain receive the reward of His suffering!"

And we pray that He truly may!!

204

EPILOGUE

Perhaps you have read this book and it has answered many of your questions. But there is a question that we would like to ask you, dear Reader, at this moment:

Have you ever given your life to Christ?

You may belong to a church or some religious organization, but the issue is more personal. The Blood of Christ only washes away your sins IF YOU have gone to Him in repentance and asked Him to cleanse you.

John 3:16 says: *"For God so loved the world, that he gave his only begotten Son, that whosoever believeth in him should not perish, but have everlasting life. For God sent not his Son into the world to condemn the world; but that the world through him might be saved."*

Jesus Christ wants not only to save you from sin and its consequences of hell, but He also wants to be Lord of your life.

If God is speaking to you now, please pray the following prayer from your heart:

"Dear Lord Jesus Christ, I repent of my sin, come into my life and wash me in Your Blood. I want to be in Covenant with You. I want to be a Child of God and I want you to be Lord of My life."

God made you to fulfill a beautiful divine purpose, discover this purpose by asking Christ to reveal Himself to you. He loves you more than you can know. Learn about Him through reading and meditating on His Word and spending time talking to Him in prayer. He is always ready to listen.

I will be praying for you!

Rona Spiropoulos

For speaking engagements contact:

Rona Spiropoulos
PO Box 447
Jasper, Arkansas 72641

Email: rona@eth-s.org